THE HISTORY OF
AIRCRAFT CARRIERS

THE HISTORY OF
AIRCRAFT CARRIERS

AN AUTHORITATIVE GUIDE TO 100 YEARS OF AIRCRAFT CARRIER DEVELOPMENT, FROM
THE FIRST FLIGHTS FROM SHIPS IN THE EARLY 1900s THROUGH TO THE PRESENT DAY

BERNARD IRELAND

southwater

This edition is published by Southwater
an imprint of Anness Publishing Ltd
Hermes House, 88–89 Blackfriars Road, London SE1 8HA
tel. 020 7401 2077; fax 020 7633 9499

www.southwaterbooks.com; www.annesspublishing.com

Anness Publishing has a new picture agency outlet for images for publishing, promotions
or advertising. Please visit our website www.practicalpictures.com for more information.

UK agent: The Manning Partnership Ltd,
tel. 01225 478444;
fax 01225 478440;
sales@manning-partnership.co.uk

UK distributor: Grantham Book
Services Ltd,
tel. 01476 541080;
fax 01476 541061;
orders@gbs.tbs-ltd.co.uk

North American agent/distributor:
National Book Network, tel. 301 459 3366;
fax 301 429 5746; www.nbnbooks.com

Australian agent/distributor: Pan Macmillan Australia,
tel. 1300 135 113; fax 1300 135 103;
customer.service@macmillan.com.au

New Zealand agent/distributor: David Bateman Ltd,
tel. (09) 415 7664; fax (09) 415 8892

Publisher: Joanna Lorenz
Senior Managing Editor: Conor Kilgallon
Senior Editor: Felicity Forster
Cover Design: Balley Design Associates
Designer: Design Principals
Copy Editor and Indexer: Tim Ellerby
Production Controller: Claire Rae

ETHICAL TRADING POLICY
At Anness Publishing we believe that business should be conducted in an ethical and ecologically
sustainable way, with respect for the environment and a proper regard to the replacement of the natural
resources we employ. As a publisher, we use a lot of high-quality paper for printing, mostly made from
spruce trees. We are therefore currently growing more than 500,000 trees in two Scottish forest
plantations near Aberdeen – Berrymoss (130 hectares/320 acres) and West Touxhill (125 hectares/305
acres). The forests we manage contain twice the number of trees employed each year in paper-making
for our books. Because of this ongoing ecological investment programme, you, as our customer, can
have the pleasure and reassurance of knowing that a tree is being cultivated on your behalf to naturally
replace the materials used to make the book you are holding. Our forestry programme is run in
accordance with the UK Woodland Assurance Scheme (UKWAS) and will be certified by the
internationally recognized Forest Stewardship Council (FSC). The FSC is a non-government organization
dedicated to promoting responsible management of the world's forests. Certification ensures forests are
managed in an environmentally sustainable and socially responsible way. For further information about
this scheme, go to www.annesspublishing.com/trees.

A CIP catalogue record for this book is available from the British Library.

Previously published as part of a larger volume, *Aircraft Carriers*

1 3 5 7 9 10 8 6 4 2

PAGE 1: *Melbourne.* PAGE 2: *Invincible.* PAGE 3: *Ark Royal* **(I)**. PAGE 5: *Illustrious.*

Contents

6 Introduction

8 First flights from ships
10 Zeppelins
12 Seaplanes versus landplanes
14 The Dardanelles Campaign
16 Fighters aboard ships
18 Air-dropped torpedoes
20 The *Königsberg* operation
22 Naval aviation at Jutland
24 The first naval air strikes
26 British shipborne aircraft of
World War I
28 Rigid airships after World War I
30 The Sempill mission and
Japanese naval aviation
32 The Washington Treaties (1921–22)
34 Carrier operational philosophies
36 "Billy" Mitchell and the US Navy
bombing trials
38 Catapults and arresters
40 Aircraft aboard submarines
42 Inter-war development in
carrier aircraft
44 Armoured versus "open" construction
46 Taranto
48 The *Bismarck* operation

50 The Battle of Matapan
52 Pearl Harbor
54 The Doolittle Raid and the
Battle of the Coral Sea
56 The Battle of Midway
58 Escort carriers
60 Carrier aircraft development
during World War II
62 The Battle of Santa Cruz
64 Battle of the Philippine Sea
66 Leyte Gulf
68 Post-war aircraft carrier developments
70 Carriers in the Korean War
72 Carriers for sale
74 Suez
76 The impact of helicopters
78 Carrier jet aircraft developments
80 Naval air power in Vietnam
82 Carrier battle groups and tactics
84 The introduction of V/STOL
86 Argument – large or small carriers?
88 Assault carriers
90 Carriers in the Falklands War

92 Glossary
94 Index
96 Acknowledgements

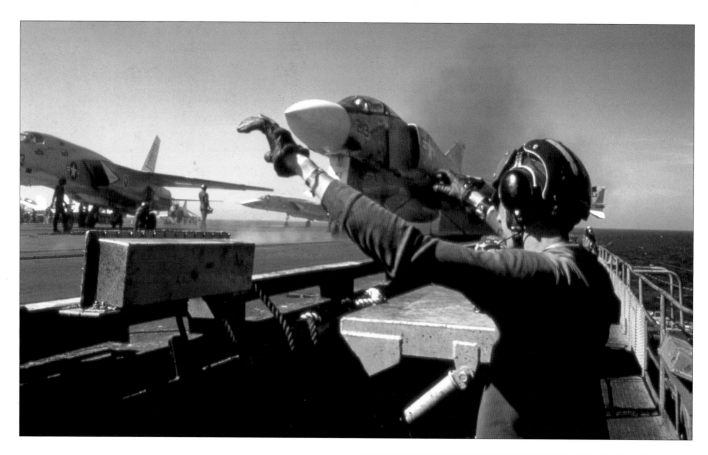

Introduction

At the time of writing, it is over 100 years since Orville Wright provided "the proof which actual flight alone can give ... [that] an engine-driven, man-carrying aerodrome [sic] had been constructed", at Kitty Hawk, North Carolina, USA. The flight inspired a rash of fabric and baling-wire contraptions that vied with lighter-than-air craft to establish mastery in the art of free flight.

Within five years, brave young men were demonstrating to their respective navies that these fragile machines could actually be flown to and from warships. Although deeply sceptical as to whether they could survive the rough and tumble of life at sea, and at the significant impact that their presence had on a ship, senior officers viewed aircraft with considerable interest. The promise of being able to loft a pair of keen eyes to several thousand feet to observe the movements of the opponent was the dream of every admiral, so it was a promise worth pursuing.

For the British Royal Navy, Admiral Fisher's dictum had been simply "Hit first, hit hard and keep hitting" which, in the days before radar and reliable fire control, was not easy to satisfy. If an airborne observer could report enemy movement, he could equally well report fall of shot to enable his admiral to get on target just that little bit more quickly.

From duelling with pistols, pilots quickly progressed to hand-dropped bombs but knew that the difference between this and toting a torpedo was only a matter of lift and engine power.

TOP: **A green-vested member of the catapult crew seems to be conducting the aircraft waiting to take off USS *Constellation* (CVA-64) in the South China Sea off Vietnam. Nearest is an F-4 Phantom while inboard and to the stern are RA-5C Vigilantes.** ABOVE: **The first of many, Britain's *Argus* (I), 1918, pioneered the functional combination of a "through flight deck" that was served by elevators connecting with the hangar below.**

Wartime development was rapid. In 1914, aircraft were still being set afloat to begin and end their flight. Four years later HMS *Argus* introduced the world to the through-deck aircraft carrier, a vessel of functional ugliness but of undoubted utility.

Before the peace, the Royal Navy lost the huge reserve of innovation and enthusiasm that had created the first-ever effective air arm, when it was transferred to the new, unified air force. During the inter-war years the Fleet Air Arm lapsed into near mediocrity compared with its major peers in the American and Japanese fleets. The Royal Navy deployed naval aviation in modest strength, its main objective being to injure and slow down a reluctant enemy enough to bring him within range of the fleet's heavy guns. Although, in this, it enjoyed some success, the other fleets were better appreciating the advantage of the big air wing, with its potential to deliver

ABOVE: **The Japanese carrier** *Zuikaku*, **together with her sister,** *Shokaku*, **spearheaded the task group that demonstrated, early in 1942, the potency of massed seaborne airstrikes.** RIGHT: **Although influential as the first "third generation" British carrier,** *Ark Royal* **(II) was a one-off. Her successors traded aircraft capacity for improved horizontal protection.**

overwhelming short-term force at a selected point. In this, they were far closer to adhering to Fisher's expressed aims.

World War II proved the concept of the deck-load air strike, confirming the carrier as the undisputed capital ship. However, many war-built vessels were soon rendered obsolescent as developments continued apace – jet propulsion, atomic weapons, angled decks and steam catapults, and finally nuclear propulsion.

Other fleets also deployed carriers and naval aviation, but for the most part discovered that the costs were not offset by the advantages. In the Royal Navy, naval aviation was only saved from oblivion because of the fortuitous introduction of Vertical or Short Take-Off and Land (V/STOL) aircraft. However, carriers that are configured to deploy V/STOL aircraft and helicopters are no substitute for "real" carriers.

The Americans, with their steadily diminishing number of carrier battle groups, are now virtually alone in being able to influence local events around the world by simply appearing in strength offshore. Such a latent threat, the contemporary equivalent of "gunboat diplomacy", is fully mobile, deployable at short notice anywhere that ships can float, and independent of costly, vulnerable and generally unpopular overseas bases.

From time to time, the large carrier, like the tank, has been written off as too vulnerable to survive in a missile-dominated battle environment. Like the tank, however, it continues to thrive and evolve, simply because there is nothing to replace it.

This book is organized chronologically, taking the reader on a historical journey from the first flights from ships in the 1900s, through the Dardanelles Campaign and World War I to Pearl Harbor, Korea, Suez, Vietnam, the Falklands War and beyond.

BELOW: **The embodiment of seapower, virtually unchallengeable by conventional means, American carrier groups have enjoyed a half-century of dominance at sea.** RIGHT: **Vast geopolitical changes near the end of the 20th century obliged major armed forces to redefine their missions. For the Royal Navy the big carrier made its comeback with the first of a new generation.**

First flights from ships

Observing Glenn Curtiss demonstrating aircraft to the US Army in 1908, naval officers were moved to suggest putting one aboard a warship, as yet for no clear purpose. Enthusiasm for flying was general at this time and an American newspaper offered a substantial prize for the first pilot to fly from a ship to a point ashore. The German HAPAG line took up the challenge but, as it happened, its failed attempt in November 1910 was upstaged by the US Navy, which had quietly been preparing its own.

Two months later, Captain Washington Irving Chambers had been appointed to liaise and cooperate with the experimenters. With modest funding he was able to engage Eugene Ely, an associate of Curtiss, to undertake a flight from a warship.

A temporary ramp, sloping downward from bridge to stemhead, was built over the forecastle of the scout cruiser USS *Birmingham* and, on November 14, 1910, Ely opened the throttle and launched himself into history. In gusty conditions, his wheeled undercarriage brushed the surface, but he recovered to fly the 3.2km/2 miles to shore.

Witnessing the feat, the acting Secretary of the Navy deemed it good publicity, immediately supporting a proposal to undertake the more difficult exercise of landing-on.

A temporary wooden platform was laid over the quarterdeck of the armoured cruiser *Pennsylvania*. It was complete with refinements such as "round-down" and a score of transverse ropes, weighted with sandbags, to arrest the aircraft. On January 18, 1911, Ely duly landed-on, remaining aboard for

TOP: **The first aircraft purchased for the US Navy, the Triad (A-1) being tested at Hammondsport by its designer Glenn Curtiss and Lt Theodore G. Ellyson, who was to become naval aviator No. 1. Able to operate from both water and land with its floats and wheels, the Triad was the first successful amphibian.** ABOVE: **Eugene Ely gets airborne from the deck of the USS *Birmingham* at Hampton Roads, Virginia on November 14, 1910. The historic first flight from ship to shore was about 3.2km/2 miles.**

an hour before "doing the double" by taking off again and flying ashore. Both *Birmingham* and *Pennsylvania* had been anchored.

In Europe, the British Admiralty, aware of activity on the part of both the French and Russian navies, had been training a first party of volunteer pilots through the good offices of the Royal Aero Club at Eastchurch, near Sheerness, and under the benevolent eye of the innovative then First Lord, Winston Churchill. The first two students gained their proficiency certification in April 1911. One of them, Charles Rumney Samson, not only taught Churchill himself to fly but went on to make the first flight from a British warship.

An inter-service committee had been considering the potential of aviation, the Royal Navy seeing its function as being to observe blockaded enemy harbours, "to ascend from a floating base" to scout for enemy forces at sea, to spot enemy submarines and minefields, and to direct naval gunfire.

Curtiss made a first flight in his "hydro-aeroplane" in February 1911 (the French had done it in 1910), the aircraft being symbolically hoisted by crane aboard the *Pennsylvania*. Two naval pilots, Schwann and Longmore, made the first British seaplane take-offs later in 1911.

During November 1911, Samson flew a Short S.27 off the forecastle ramp of the battleship *Africa* at a buoy off Sheerness. He used the same aircraft again in May 1912 for the next demonstration, staged during a Royal Fleet Review at Portland. Here, he made the first-ever take-off from a ship under weigh, flying from the battleship *Hibernia* to release a simulated 45kg/100lb bomb. Two months later, he made a similar flight from the battleship *London*, proceeding at 12 knots.

In the United States, the successes with Curtiss' wheeled aircraft had encouraged Chambers to talk in terms of "platform ships", i.e. with flight decks, but the growing potential of seaplanes sidetracked him from what would have been a promising direction of development.

TOP: **One of the great pioneers of manned flight, Glen H. Curtiss is seen here having just completed his record-making flight from Albany to New York in June 1910. He was to tell an interviewer, "Some day soon aeroplanes will have to start from the deck of battleships …"** ABOVE: **A Short S.38 on the flying-off platform of HMS *Africa*. Reports, unconfirmed, state that Charles Rumney Samson made the first British flight from the *Africa* in December 1911.**
LEFT: **The first recorded flight by Samson from HMS *Africa*, on January 19, 1912.**

ABOVE: **Watched by crewmen crowding every vantage point, Eugene Ely makes the first ever touchdown on a warship's deck. The USS *Pennsylvania* was anchored off San Francisco on January 18, 1911.**

Zeppelins

The primary roles envisaged for early, low-powered heavier-than-air craft were based on observation and reconnaissance. In these, they were still inferior in many respects to lighter-than-air craft. Of these, the simplest were the tethered aerostats, of which the most common were kite balloons, deployed by many warships and auxiliaries.

Powered airships, capable of navigation, were properly termed "dirigibles". Those with an internal frame were termed "rigid", those without, "non-rigid". The latter, like balloons, were little more than inflated gas bags, and limited in size. As the British failed to master the technology of the rigid airship, they operated considerable numbers of non-rigids, popularly called "blimps". In naval service, their small size restricted them largely to coastal duties.

The most dominant airship was the large rigid, a category which, until after World War I, was virtually synonymous with "Zeppelin". These craft stemmed from the Friedrichshafen factory established by Graf Ferdinand von Zeppelin in 1898 to promote popular air travel as well as construct "air cruisers" for national defence.

Despite early setbacks and rivalry with the Schütte-Lanz company, Zeppelin's machines had been acquired for the German army by 1910 and, two years later, for the navy. Zeppelin had met the army's requirement for an operational endurance of 24 hours and it was this, together with its potential in long-range reconnaissance, which attracted naval interest. The placing of the naval order was, however, the

ABOVE: **Count von Zeppelin's main intention was to use his machines to popularize air travel. This pre-war impression emphasizes the more idyllic aspect of his enterprise.**

ABOVE: **An Italian non-rigid DE-type scouting airship communicating with an anti-submarine motor boat, or MAS. Of a total of 49 airships, the Italians lost seven in the course of the war, two of them as a result of accidents.**
LEFT: **With a volume of nearly 56,000m³/2,000,000cu ft, the L.53 was one of the largest types of Zeppelin to see service. She was a victim of an RNAS Camel fighter, flown from a high-speed lighter on August 11, 1918.**

effective end of Zeppelin's personal direction of company affairs. He was not a trained engineer and, with the navy insisting on imposing its own constructors and naval architects to improve and enlarge his products, he lost interest. By the outbreak of war in 1914, the Zeppelin Company was virtually a state concern.

The Royal Navy's airship aspirations were effectively wrecked along with its prototype rigid in 1911. This failure was exacerbated by Admiral Sir John Jellicoe (soon to become C-in-C, Grand Fleet) and Captain Murray Sueter (Director, Admiralty Air Department) separately travelling as civilians in commercial flights by Zeppelins and returning enthused with the craft's potential.

Lacking a similar force, it is perhaps not surprising that the Royal Navy, during the course of its North Sea operations of World War I, developed a phobia known commonly as "Zeppelinitis". Symptoms were widespread and took the form of a conviction that the fleet's every move was being observed. The truth was quite different as Admiral Tirpitz, father of the Imperial Navy, distrusted new technologies and was little interested in anything but his battle fleet. Fortunately for the British, he had neglected both the submarine arm and the Naval Airship Division, both of which began their war seriously below the approved establishment.

In the Royal Navy, long-range, high-angle, anti-aircraft gunnery was still in its infancy. The only true antidote to the Zeppelin was therefore the high-performance fighter for, by dumping ballast, the airship had a rate of climb which left it immune to interception by anything else unless surprised or otherwise caught unawares.

As a result the Zeppelin was the primary catalyst in the protracted and innovative process by which the Royal Navy produced the world's first through-deck aircraft carrier.

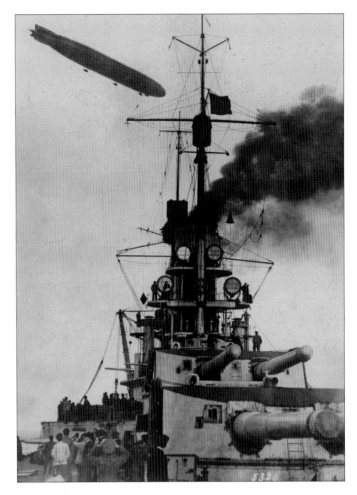

In practice, too many Zeppelins were diverted to unprofitable and costly bombing raids on England, while those allocated to fleet operation proved to be hostage to weather conditions. Requiring enormous dimensions for a modest payload, the airship eventually proved to be an evolutionary dead-end, the aircraft proving to be much more efficient.

TOP: **During operations in the Baltic, a reconnaissance Zeppelin overflies a German battleship, probably the *Markgraf*. BELOW: Another of the largest Zeppelins, the L.45 is here seen above two of the three sheds at Tondern. She was lost through forced-landing in France in October 1917.**

ABOVE: **A small, early example of a Zeppelin, L.9 had a volume of about 25,000m³/880,000cu ft and a length of 161.2m/529.3ft comparable with that of the armoured cruiser *Blücher*.**

Seaplanes versus landplanes

In February 1911, a month after Eugene Ely had shown that it was possible to land a landplane on a warship, Glenn Curtiss successfully took off in his "hydro-aeroplane", landed alongside the *Pennsylvania* and was briefly craned aboard. This then begged the question of which type of aircraft offered most for future progress. Superficially, the choice appeared simple. Take-off and landing platforms for landplanes were unwieldy and affected a warship's fighting power. On the other hand, a seaplane (as it came to be called) needed only to be transported, the water surface anywhere being its operating platform. This was attractive as an option but, perversely the sea is rarely calm and the aircraft was fragile. Further, its cumbersome float's and high undercarriage guaranteed that its performance would be inferior to that of an equivalent landplane.

From the outset, the Americans regarded the development of the catapult as a means to minimize the impact of aircraft on the launching ship. Their first successful launch of a seaplane from an improvised compressed air model occurred in November 1912, followed a month later by the launch of one of Curtiss' small flying boats. A practical catapult might be located more conveniently on a warship, but this still left unresolved the problem of alighting and recovery.

The British showed little initial enthusiasm for catapults and it was not until 1916 that they modified an Admiralty hopper, renamed *Slinger*, to conduct practical trials. For them, the

TOP: **Seen at Mitylene during the Dardanelles campaign, the *Ark Royal* (I) has a Short 166 "on the hook". Although designed to carry a 356mm/14in torpedo, the aircraft was capable of only 105kph/65mph. Note the Union Flag marking that pre-dated the familiar roundel.** ABOVE: **Originally an engines-aft, steam-driven hopper, the *Slinger* was converted for trials with catapults. Trials were suspended in 1919 as aircraft of the time took off equally well from a simple platform.**

simple, if ungainly, launching platform sufficed. As the average aircraft of the time could rise almost vertically from a standing position in as little as 45 knots relative wind speed, fast ships such as light cruisers needed no more than a platform. Capital ships began by locating platforms atop gun turrets, which could be trained to avoid having to steam into the wind.

The seaplane, launched on an expendable trolley and recovered from the sea, gave way to a wheeled landplane of higher performance, which alighted on the surface with the aid of temporary flotation bags.

It was obvious to all, however, that the ideal lay in a ship configured to both launch and recover wheeled aircraft. Even as the Americans were making their first successful catapult launches, the Beardmore yard approached the British Admiralty with proposals for a 15,000-tonner with sided superstructures and a straight-through deck along its central axis. Capable of accommodating, launching and recovering aircraft, she might have been the first true carrier had the Admiralty been bolder.

Instead, the small cruiser HMS *Hermes* was modified early in 1913 with a take-off ramp and canvas "hangars" for two seaplanes, a French Caudron G. III and a British Short S.64, the latter already fitted with folding wings and a radio. During fleet manoeuvres of 1913 the *Hermes* staged over thirty successful flights, demonstrating that seaplanes, at least, could be deployed at sea on a sustained basis. This led directly to the Admiralty acquiring a hull capable of being remodelled into a specialist seaplane carrier. It was this ship that was completed in 1914 as *Ark Royal* (I).

Up to this point the French had, if anything, been slightly ahead with their conversion of the *Foudre*, while the Japanese had modified the *Wakamiya* to operate a mix of British and French-built seaplanes.

ABOVE: **The Italian Navy constructed several big-gun monitors to bombard Austrian shore installations. Dating from mid-1917 the *Faà di Bruno*, shown here being directed by a flying boat, boasted two 381mm/15in guns on a displacement of only 2,854 tonnes/2,809 tons.** BELOW: **First of the Royal Navy's seaplane-carrier conversions, the cruiser *Hermes* was, in 1913, given a launch platform forward and a canvas hangar aft. She is seen sinking after having been torpedoed in October 1914, the remains of the seaplane on her quarterdeck clearly visible.**

ABOVE: **One of three Gotha WD 20s built for long-range reconnaissance flight for the German Navy. Developed from the WD 14 torpedo-bomber, the WD 20 swapped weapon load for additional fuel to give it up to 10 hours of endurance.** LEFT: **Glenn Curtiss, having successfully flown his first flying boat early in 1912, developed his designs through a series of early prototypes. The F-Type, seen here, typifies the flimsy nature of early models.**

The Dardanelles Campaign

Strategically brilliant but tactically inept, the Dardanelles campaign of 1915 quickly mired into static warfare. Considerable Allied military forces were confined to the Gallipoli peninsula, where they were totally dependent upon support by sea. During the ten-or-so months of the campaign, the fleets were based on nearby islands.

The newly-completed *Ark Royal* (I), with six seaplanes, was involved from the outset but, although lacking nothing in enthusiasm, the infant Royal Naval Air Squadron (RNAS), was as the service expression has it, "thrown in at the deep end". During the initial naval bombardments, her aircraft were able to reconnoitre the many enemy fortifications but the boisterous February weather caused many flights to be aborted.

Hopes for the forts' destruction rested much on the 381mm/15in guns of the new battleship *Queen Elizabeth*. This was to be achieved through indirect fire across the peninsula, with fall of shot being corrected from the air. However, no trained observers yet existed (a midshipman was usually selected on the basis of being the lightest!), and communications proved unreliable as no time had been

TOP: **HMS *Ark Royal* (I) is seen here soon after her arrival at Mudros in March 1915. The space abaft the cranes marks the hangar access hatch, while the long, unencumbered foredeck was intended for take-offs, although never used as such.** ABOVE: **Great things were expected from bombardment by HMS *Queen Elizabeth*'s 381mm/15in guns. Aerial spotting proved difficult, however, due to shortcomings in both aircraft and communications.**

allowed for testing, training or rehearsal. When aloft, the under-powered aircraft had to fly so low that they were continually struck by rifle fire.

In June 1915, the *Ark Royal* was relieved by the *Ben-my-Chree*, but for her the hot summer weather created its own problems. Seaplanes found it difficult to "unstick" from glassy water in the absence of wind, while the ever-present dust tormented already temperamental engines. Fortunately, enemy aircraft were few, however those that did appear were landplanes of higher performance and regularly reconnoitred the main fleet base at Mudros. "One of our lumbering seaplanes went up after it like an owl in sunlight" it was recorded, "but could rise no higher than the masts of the Fleet".

By dint of the round-the-clock efforts from its artificers, the RNAS averaged ten to twelve sorties daily, usually eight devoted to bombing (a Short 184 could lift 236kg/520lb) or

ABOVE: **One of the *Ark Royal* (I)'s Short 166 seaplanes is seen here taxiing across the harbour at Mudros. Note that the roundel marking has been adopted. The harbour was always packed with merchant shipping carrying naval supplies.**

spotting for naval gunfire, and only two to reconnaissance, for which just one modern camera was available.

There was an obvious need for higher-performance landplanes. However, because there was no point on the peninsula secure from enemy artillery fire, these had to operate from Mudros, which allowed them little time over Gallipoli.

During the initial landings and any littoral operations, the kite balloon proved to be more reliable for observation. However, even with their ship anchored close inshore the useful range of observation was limited. Their telephonic links were reliable, and despite their crews suffering badly from motion sickness, they usefully directed naval gunfire. In addition to those deployed by warships, there were those from the balloon ship *Manica*, later relieved by the *Hector*.

Great hopes had been placed on spotting enemy minefields from aircraft but conditions made this impossible. Known fields could not be swept because they were covered by artillery and unknown, short-term fields wreaked considerable execution.

A "first" achieved by the *Ben-my-Chree*'s Short 184s during August 1915, was the torpedoing and destruction of two enemy merchantmen in the strait.

Overall, naval aviation at the Dardanelles was poorly rated by the Admiralty, but this was due in great measure to senior officers not appreciating the still-primitive nature of the technologies involved and thus failing either to husband their very limited resources or to employ them efficiently within their obvious limitations.

TOP: **Another view of Mudros, dominated by the elegant lines of a *Cressy*-class armoured cruiser, with an *Eclipse*-class protected cruiser beyond. The blimp overhead was more useful than heavier-than-air craft in spotting, but was more vulnerable to enemy ground fire.** ABOVE: **Wing Commander Charles Rumney Samson with a French-built Nieuport Two-seater of his No.3 Wing at the Dardanelles. Note the observer's upward-firing Lewis gun. The extra-warm jacket, pistol and last cigarette are also noteworthy.** LEFT: **Lightly-built and not very suitable for operations in the North Sea, the Sopwith Schneider proved effective in the eastern Mediterranean, both at the Dardanelles and in the Aegean, as seen here. The anchored brigantines evoke an age that was about to disappear.**

Fighters aboard ships

The first three channel packets converted to seaplane carriers (*Engadine*, *Empress* and *Riviera)* were equipped only with hangar space and cranes. Their aircraft were of low performance and intended for reconnaissance, spotting, and bomber/torpedo roles. Lacking any flying-off ramps, the ships were required to heave-to to both despatch and recover their seaplanes. Already slow for fleet operations, they thus incurred further delay.

Their primitive level of capability was demonstrated on Christmas Day, 1914, when the three transported a total of nine aircraft to bomb the Zeppelin base at Cuxhaven. Only seven machines took the air, one found the target but inflicted no damage, and just three aircraft returned to their ships. The raid had historical significance in that it was the first-ever seaborne air strike, attracting in return the first-ever bombing attack on a warship at sea. It also demonstrated the still-rudimentary nature of naval aviation.

Packets converted later were improved by the addition of forward flying-off ramps. Initially, these were intended for launching seaplanes with the aid of expendable trolleys. These ships were supplemented by the rebuilt ex-Cunard ship, *Campania*. Aged, and arthritic with machinery problems, she was, nonetheless, considerably larger. In place of 18–24m/ 60–80ft launching platforms, hers was 50m/165ft in length and, importantly, she could maintain her speed in a seaway.

Frustration with the limitations of seaplanes led Admiral Jellicoe, C-in-C Grand Fleet to demand that "aeroplanes", i.e. landplanes, be introduced. On November 3, 1915, the first, a Bristol Scout "C" fighter flew from the *Vindex*, starting a sequence that would evolve through the Scout "D", the Sopwith Pup, the 1½-Strutter and the Camel.

The short ramp of the *Vindex* was copied aboard half-a-dozen light cruisers, the first of which, HMS *Yarmouth*,

ABOVE: **A Sopwith 2F.2 Camel lifts easily from the short launching platform of the Australian light cruiser *Sydney*. This picture dates from the latter part of World War I, the aircraft not being carried when the ship sank the celebrated German raider *Emden* in 1914. Note the 152mm/6in gun in an open mounting.**
BELOW: **Another view of a light cruiser's launch platform. From HMS *Yarmouth*'s bridge its limited dimensions are very apparent. Note that the guard rails and jack staff support have been lowered. The aircraft is a Sopwith Pup, piloted by Squadron Commander Frederick J. Rutland.**

ABOVE: **Fifty high-speed lighters were ordered in 1917 for the transport of flying boats. Equally able to launch fighters if towed above 25 knots, 12 were thus converted. Here Flight Sub-Lieutenant Stuart Culley, who would shoot down the L.53, lifts off in a Camel while in tow by the destroyer** *Redoubt*. LEFT: **Sideslipping around the superstructure, Squadron Commander Edwin Dunning lands on** *Furious'* **foredeck, August 2, 1917. The Pup is virtually hovering, and ship's officers are racing to haul it down to deck.**

successfully flew a Pup in June 1917 from a platform just 6m/20ft in length. This feat was quickly exploited for, on August 21, a Pup from the same ship intercepted Zeppelin L.23 near Terschelling, destroying it with "10 to15 shots".

Other launching platforms appeared atop the turrets of capital ships but, at this point, with recovery dependent upon flotation bags and the situation at the time, the aircraft was still very much an expendable item. Experience with the *Campania*, however, had led to a similar conversion on the new and fast "large light cruiser" *Furious*. She entered service in July 1917 and, on August 2, Squadron Commander Edwin Dunning used the Pup's excellent low-speed characteristics to make a risky side-slip and land on the *Furious'* forward flying-off deck. A repeat proved fatal but was instrumental in the ship being further modified with an after flying-on deck.

The Sopwith 2F.1 Camel was designed specifically as a shipboard fighter and on July 17, 1918, *Furious* launched seven of them against the Tondern Zeppelin base. Two airships were destroyed with bombs. A fortnight later, a Camel took off successfully from a specifically designed lighter, towed at high speed by a destroyer of the Harwich Force. Again, the stratagem was quickly exploited, the same pilot, the 18-year-old Lieutenant S.D. Culley, employing it on August 10 to bring down the L.53. The blazing, falling Zeppelin inspired Commodore Tyrwhitt to make the memorable signal, addressed to all ships, "See Hymns Ancient and Modern, Number 224, verse 7". Due consultation confirmed this to read:

"O happy band of pilgrims,
Look upward to the skies,
Where such a light affliction
Shall win so great a prize."

ABOVE: **In a scene that foreshadows the packed flight decks of later years, six of HMS** *Furious'* **Sopwith Camels are seen ranged forward in 1918. In the foreground is the hatch-like opening of the forward elevator. Note the palisade windbreaks, their paintwork continuing the ship's striped camouflage.**
BELOW: **Still wearing her wartime dazzle paintwork in this 1917 picture, the converted packet HMS** *Pegasus* **launches a Sopwith 1½-Strutter fighter. The crew members are standing on a portable platform section that permitted aircraft to be transferred from the hangar space below the goalpost mast.**

Air-dropped torpedoes

The idea of dropping torpedoes from seaplanes originated virtually with the seaplane itself, and can be attributed to no one person.

In the United States, the innovative Bradley Fiske, then a Rear Admiral, filed a patent for an air-dropped torpedo early in 1912. Although first favouring a weapon controlled by radio from an aircraft, he moved to the sounder idea of aiming the aircraft itself, increasing the probability of success through employing several simultaneously.

During the same year, Engineer Captain Alessandro Guidoni of the Italian Navy added floats to a French Henri Farman landplane to experiment with the dropping of deadloads to the limit of the aircraft's capacity. In 1913, he was given a more powerful, twin-engined seaplane, enabling him to demonstrate dropping a dummy 375kg/827lb torpedo on February 26, 1914.

Meanwhile at the Royal Naval Air Station at Eastchurch, Captain Murray Sueter enlisted the assistance of Thomas Sopwith to construct a rig for the evaluation of torpedo release gear at high speeds. This equipment Sopwith then incorporated into his Type "C" aircraft, with which he demonstrated that carrying a 363kg/800lb, 356mm/14in torpedo was feasible in 1913. Finally, on July 28, 1914, a first live drop was made by a Short Folder.

A 356mm/14in weapon had limited hitting power and, with his eye set on larger targets, Sueter set Sopwith the task of designing a landplane able to carry a 457mm/18in weapon. The existence of this project appears in minutes dated June 25,

TOP: **Designed from the outset to carry the harder-hitting 457mm/18in torpedo, the Sopwith Cuckoo needed to be a robustly constructed landplane in order to carry the load. The torpedo's propellers are here covered by a protective cap.** ABOVE: **An interesting "nuts and bolts" view of a Cuckoo, taken from an instruction manual. Of immediate note are the sturdy undercarriage, the small volume of the engine and the obviously poor forward view enjoyed by the pilot when putting down on a carrier's deck.**

1914 (and, therefore, pre-war) and was connected with the provision and location of coastal air stations. Inter alia, these stated that "the danger of raids would be greatly reduced by the prospect of torpedo-carrying aircraft stationed 80km/ 50 miles apart all along the coast ... The detection and attack of hostile craft would be rendered much more rapid by the introduction of this type of coast defence". In view of the German fleet's shortly-to-be-adopted tactics of hit-and-run bombardments of English east coast towns, this appraisal was prescient but, unfortunately, well ahead of the technology to support it, for it would be 1917 before Sopwith could introduce the required aircraft.

The then First Lord, Winston Churchill, informed Sueter and his colleagues as early as April 3, 1915, that a very large fleet of aircraft was required. In place of individual "dashing exploits", it was necessary to deal "a decisive blow ... at the enemy's capital ships ... either in a fleet action or in his harbours".

The first successful "dashing exploits" were themselves still several months in the future, being the August 14 attacks by the *Ben-my-Chree*'s aircraft in the Dardanelles theatre.

As the British moved toward their objective of a mass torpedo attack on the German and/or Austrian fleet, the Germans themselves were not idle. By November 1916, their twin-engined Gothas were torpedoing merchant shipping off the English east coast. To lift them from the water, these aircraft required two 119kW/160bhp engines. In contrast, Sopwith's landplane, lifting from the flight decks that Sueter envisaged, required only a singe, 149kW/200bhp unit.

The Sopwith T.1 (later named the "Cuckoo") first flew in June 1917 but was a further year entering service. On October 19, 1918, the first operational squadron embarked on the new, flush-deck carrier *Argus*. Within a month the plan for the mass torpedo attack was terminated by the Armistice. By then, its gifted but outspoken champion, Murray Sueter, had joined Churchill in the dark outer regions of official favour.

TOP: **A Blackburn-built Cuckoo here makes a perfect release. Flying straight and low at about 90 knots made the aircraft vulnerable to return gunfire, however.** ABOVE: **The pioneer carrier HMS *Argus* manoeuvres in the Grand Harbour, not a straightforward task for a high-sided ship in a crosswind. Note the smoke from the problematical exhaust ducting, and the rows of scuttles, a legacy of her passenger liner origins.** LEFT: **Not driven by the same degree of urgency, the US Navy did not develop torpedo aircraft until after World War I. Here, a Liberty-engined Curtiss R-6L releases a weapon in 1922. The Curtiss R-series aircraft with floats or wheeled undercarriage, were also used by the RNAS, but in non-combat roles.** BELOW: **In what turned out to be an evolutionary dead-end Curtiss designed his Model 24 with twin engines to solve the problem of the heavy load of a torpedo. The US Navy ordered nine of the aircraft, designated the CT-1, but only one, seen here, was fitted in 1922 to actually carry a torpedo.**

The *Königsberg* operation

At the outbreak of World War I, several German cruisers were at large as commerce raiders. Operating in the Indian Ocean was the *Königsberg*, which having destroyed two ships, went to ground. On October 30, 1914, she was located by HM cruiser *Chatham*, hiding several miles inside the maze of waterways that form the delta of the Rufiji River, in what was then German East Africa.

Too deep in draught to ascend the river themselves, the *Chatham* and consorts instituted a blockade. The *Königsberg* shifted berth from time to time and, pending arrival of the promised Royal Naval Air Service (RNAS) flight, the senior British officer kept track of her through the services of a civilian pilot. From giving public exhibitions in his Curtiss "hydroplane", this gentleman found himself a temporary commission, his aircraft purchased and, with it, shipped north to the British base on Mafia Island. The aircraft's life was short but a second one was located and brought in.

Meanwhile, following rapid preparation, RNAS Expeditionary Squadron No. 4 arrived in early February 1915, together with two seaplanes and a party that included a Sopwith mechanic and a propeller expert. Presumably, the outfit also included a supply of bombs of up to 23kg/50lb. The RNAS task, however, was primarily to cooperate with naval gunners to encompass the enemy's destruction.

The agency for this was two small river monitors, *Severn* and *Mersey*, which, while drawing only 1.68m/5ft 6in of water,

TOP: **Seen here at Dar-es-Salaam, the 3,455-tonne/3,400-ton light cruiser** *Königsberg* **was the pre-war station ship for German East Africa. With war, her orders were to use these territories as a base and to act against allied shipping in the Indian Ocean. Having achieved little, however, she inexplicably "went to ground" in the remote and inaccessible Rufiji delta.** ABOVE: **Blockaded by the British, the** *Königsberg's* **commanding officer established observation posts and gun positions along the approaches. Colonial duties at the time demanded innovative personnel and** *Königsberg* **crew are here seen manning a strongpoint.**

mounted two 152mm/6in guns and two 119mm/4.7in howitzers apiece. Laying in Malta, they had to be prepared and towed to East Africa, not arriving until early June.

In the interim, the RNAS had found that in the humid heat their aircraft could get aloft with only the pilot aboard and no observer, bombs, and a minimum amount of fuel. Even then,

ABOVE: **The blockading forces made considerable use of aircraft for tracking the *Königsberg*'s movements and, finally, for spotting. They proved to be highly unreliable in the humid climate and here what appears to be a Short 827/830 is being towed by HMS *Severn*, one of the two small river monitors involved.** ABOVE LEFT: **One of the Short 827s of the expedition. Note the conspicuous top-mounted radiator and the forest of wire necessary to stiffen the large span of the wings.**

they could only be coaxed to an altitude of 457m/1,500ft. Wooden propellers also warped and one aircraft was soon wrecked in a heavy landing. The other simply disintegrated as glue, rubber, and fabric failed in the conditions.

On April 23, three Short seaplanes were unloaded but these, too, were unable to climb sufficiently and all suffered damage from enemy fire; one being shot down.

Following the arrival of the monitors on June 3, four more aircraft were delivered, two Caudrons and two Henri Farmans. All were landplanes and had to be landed over the beach before being manhandled 2.4km/1.5 miles to an improvised air strip hacked out of the jungle by the now considerably enlarged RNAS party and native labour. The machines proved able to attain 1,219m/4,000ft but, again, two were soon lost.

On July 6 the monitors entered the river and, assisted by spotting aircraft, fired indirectly across the jungle. The enemy had long since established observation posts and a lively return fire ensued. Aircraft corrected about 80 of the 600-odd rounds fired by the British, who made three hits, suffering two in return.

Following repair, the monitors returned on July 11, and, after two hours and 200 more rounds, the Germans, low on ammunition, recognized the hopelessness of their situation, and scuttled their ship. Ironically, one of her final shots had brought down the sole remaining spotting aircraft, whose crew was rescued by the *Mersey*.

ABOVE LEFT: **Before the *Königsberg* affair, the Germans drafted Bruno Buckner and his Pfalz-built Otto biplane into military service, shown here with Askari guard.** ABOVE: **Obsolete even by 1914 standards, this German floatplane could have operated under only ideal conditions.** BELOW: **With no prospect of escape and being systematically reduced by British indirect gunfire, the *Königsberg* was blown up by her own crew. The "petalling" of the shell plating around the two large nearer holes indicate that they were caused by internal explosions.**

Arthur Balfour, Churchill's successor as First Lord, later felt able to announce (perhaps a trifle generously) to the War Committee that "the destruction of the *Königsberg* had been due almost entirely to the spotting of Naval aeroplanes".

Naval aviation at Jutland

The long-awaited trial of strength between the British Grand Fleet and the German High Seas Fleet finally came about off Jutland on May 31, 1916. For the former it proved to be a catalogue of disappointment and missed opportunity. On a day of fickle visibility, more and better aerial reconnaissance might well have made a significant difference to the outcome but, in truth, naval aviation was yet too fragile for such a major responsibility.

Admiral Jellicoe's Grand Fleet still had only the *Campania* and *Engadine* for air support and, farcically, the former failed to receive the signal to sail. Incorrectly assumed to be too slow to catch up, she and her ten seaplanes were ordered to remain at Scapa.

The action developed with the battle-cruiser squadrons of Beatty and Hipper heading for each other. Beatty had *Engadine* in company but, aware of the frailties of her aircraft, he refused to commit them to general reconnaissance. Only when the opposing cruiser screens had come into contact was the *Engadine* ordered to put up an aircraft. At 15:08 hours, therefore, "Seaplane No.8359" (a Short 184) took off to make history as the first aircraft to be involved in a naval battle. The pilot, Flight Lieutenant F.J. Rutland, was thereafter known widely as "Rutland of Jutland", and would go on to make a name in naval aviation.

With the cloudbase in places down to 274m/900ft and visibility of 1.6-6km/1-4 miles, Rutland had to get uncomfortably close to the enemy, attracting shrapnel bursts. His observer was able to radio one of the enemy cruisers'

TOP: **What with ineffective anti-aircraft fire and hopelessly inadequate bombs, ships and aircraft of World War I posed little mutual threat.** ABOVE: **Converted from a cross-channel packet, the seaplane carrier HMS *Engadine* became the first warship to launch an aircraft in the course of a naval action. One of her Short 184s is here visible abaft the box-like hangar.**

course changes before, at 15:45 hours, "a petrol pipe leading to the left carburretter [sic] broke". Forced to alight, Rutland "made good the defect with rubber tube" and reported that he could continue, only to be recalled by his ship.

Already too slow to remain in contact with Beatty's hard-pressed squadron, the *Engadine* now completely lost touch with it and played no further active part in the action (although she would encounter the stricken armoured cruiser *Warrior* and, unable to prevent her foundering, took off her entire surviving crew).

Admiral Scheer, commanding the German High Seas Fleet, enjoyed little better support from the Naval Airship Division. His thrust into the North Sea was to have been preceded by a line of five Zeppelins, scouting in a bold arc from southern Norway to a point off East Anglia. Poor visibility and crosswinds so delayed their departure, however, that none would observe any aspect of the daylight action of May 31.

Bent on returning to Wilhelmshaven, Scheer's fleet broke through the tail of Jellicoe's forces during the ensuing night. This triggered a series of desperately fought skirmishes, observed by at least two of a second group of five airships ordered out at dusk. Another, L.11, discovered Jellicoe's main body in the early light of June 1. For about 100 minutes, she held contact, coming under fire from all calibres of gun, at one stage from over 20 ships simultaneously. The bombardment by the frustrated British included main battery fire – "the line of ships could be made out from the muzzle flashes when the ships themselves were invisible". L.11 was not hit but "the

ABOVE LEFT: **Beyond his epic flight at Jutland, Frederick Rutland was decorated for gallantry. His later career was clouded through his subversion by the Japanese and his eventual suicide.** TOP: **Short 184 No. 8359, "the aircraft that flew at Jutland", is here seen alongside her mother ship, HMS** *Engadine*. **Parts of the original aircraft survive to this day at the Fleet Air Arm Museum, Yeovilton.** ABOVE: **A German propaganda postcard purporting to show a British battle cruiser under fire at Jutland.**

passage of the big shells and the bursting of shrapnel nearby caused such heavy vibrations in the framework that it seemed advisable to increase the distance..."

Zeppelin L.11 was, therefore, the only aircraft to contribute significantly to the operation. It is a misfortune of history that, by then, the action was over.

LEFT: **Jutland was, for the British, a material defeat. Realizing, however, that they could never defeat the Grand Fleet in battle, the German High Command was forced to resort to submarine warfare. It was the brutality of this that brought the United States, following several warnings, into World War I. This, on top of privations resulting from the British naval blockade, reduced Germany to despair, revolution and, ultimately, defeat.**

The first naval air strikes

Probably because they themselves lacked experience of large rigids, the British overestimated the capabilities of German Zeppelins, both in reconnaissance and in their capacity to inflict targeted damage by bombing. The scale of the Zeppelin "bogey" is evident in the resources devoted by both the Royal Naval Air Service (RNAS) and the Royal Flying Corps (RFC) in dealing with it.

Thus, on October 25, 1914, not three months into the war, the Harwich Force crept deeply into the Heligoland Bight in order to cover its seaplane carriers, whose objective was the Zeppelin base at Nordholz, near Cuxhaven. A heavy rainstorm was sufficient to prevent their seaplanes rising from water, however and, disgusted at the outcome ("I am sick to death of everything connected with aviation…", wrote Commodore Tyrwhitt to his wife) the force was obliged to withdraw. Taking a broader view, Churchill, the First Lord, noted, "It is no use trying these enterprises with overloaded machines. Either aeroplanes or seaplanes with wheels instead of floats must be used." Probably in these few words lay the genesis of the true aircraft carrier.

As Tyrwhitt awaited a further opportunity, a flight of RNAS landplanes was moved to Belfort whence, on November 21, they flew the 193km/120 miles to the Zeppelin works at Friedrichshafen. Their 9kg/20lb bombs narrowly failed to destroy the new L.7.

On Christmas Day 1914, the Harwich Force was again in the Heligoland Bight where, in totally calm conditions, the three seaplane carriers (*Empress*, *Engadine* and *Riviera*) hoisted out nine aircraft, all Shorts, but of three types. Only seven were

TOP: **Completed in July 1916, the Zeppelin L.31 had a life of just 12 weeks, being shot down by a British fighter. The latter's pilot reported her engulfed in flames, and just evading her "as she shot past me, roaring like a furnace".**
ABOVE: **Bomb damage inflicted upon innocent homes by Zeppelins, as here in Kings Lynn, aroused national anger.**

able to take off and these encountered fog and low cloud over the target area. Just one aircraft located the Nordholz site and its bombs caused no damage.

Nonetheless, the presence offshore of a powerful British force caused considerable German consternation. Tyrwhitt's waiting ships came under bombing and machine gun attack from two seaplanes and a Zeppelin. This, the first example of air attack on hostile warships at sea, caused some excitement but, again, no damage. Extended beyond their endurance, however, only two of the British raiders returned, although the missing crews were eventually recovered.

These disappointments set the tone for other attempts. As Churchill had observed, what was required was to operate landplanes directly from a ship's deck, implicitly with the necessary facilities for landing them on again. However, the development and provision of such would take time.

As an interim measure, the new "large light cruiser" *Furious* was converted in two stages. Between March 1917 and March 1918 she acquired a 69m/228ft flying-off deck forward and a 87m/284ft landing-on deck aft. With hangar space below for up to 16 landplanes, elevators and a rudimentary arrester system, she embodied the major features of a true aircraft carrier, although turbulence from the remaining superstructure left the landing deck too hazardous to use.

By 1918, ever-larger Zeppelins were able to carry 3.01 tonnes/ 3 tons of bombs, the largest of 300kg/661lb. Raids on England were becoming increasingly damaging and public indignation ran high. The Navy, under pressure to "do something", was now able to deploy the *Furious* against the more-distant Zeppelin facility at Tondern in Schleswig-Holstein.

On July 19, 1918, she duly despatched seven, bomb-armed Sopwith 2F.1 Camels in two flights, separated by ten minutes. The first arrived at 04:30 hours, achieving complete surprise. Two Zeppelins, L.54 and L.60, together with an aerostat, were destroyed by 23kg/50lb bombs. It was history's first successful naval air strike.

ABOVE: **Zeppelins were the direct stimulus for the extraordinary efforts made by the Royal Navy to take high-performance fighter aircraft to sea. Here, ship's routine goes on beside three Sopwith Camels ranged on the foredeck of HMS *Furious*.**
LEFT: **HMS *Furious*' foredeck, looking aft, this time with Sopwith Pups. Note the two mercantile-style posts and derricks for hoisting aircraft from the hangar below. Elevators were fitted only in 1918.**
BELOW LEFT: **On November 21, 1914, four RNAS Avro 504s sortied from a French airfield at Belfort to bomb the Zeppelin factory at Friedrichshafen. One aircraft was lost and the small damage inflicted was outweighed by the consternation caused.**
BELOW: **The wreckage of L.54 and L.60, destroyed by *Furious*' aircraft. The airships burned without exploding and so, incredibly, their enormous shed at Tondern survived, blackened but intact.**

British shipborne aircraft of World War I

As the British nation went to war in 1914 the Royal Naval Air Service (RNAS) operated an eclectic assortment of 78 aircraft types, including 20 of landplane, 12 of seaplane and 7 of non-rigid airship. Still largely experimental, it operated from shore bases, having only in the previous year sent aircraft to sea in HMS *Hermes* for evaluation in manoeuvres.

The functions of the service which had been defined by the Admiralty were observation, scouting and spotting. These duties could be undertaken by small, two-seater seaplanes, whose presence aboard a warship caused minimal impact and which, at least in theory, could use the sea for take-off and recovery, when conditions permitted.

However, the possibilities of using aircraft as torpedo carriers demanded a second category of larger seaplane for, with the low-powered engines available, the accommodation of such a load required far greater wing areas to provide the necessary lift.

From the outset, much of the RNAS' resources were mobilized to assist those of the Royal Flying Corps (RFC) in the defence of home soil against incursions by Zeppelin airships. Operations were, of course, land-based, using high-performance landplanes. Therefore, when the same Zeppelins began to dog the fleet in an observational role, the RNAS turned to solving the problems of operating landplanes from ships. A third category of aircraft had thus been added and modes of operation had been extended from neutral to both offensive and defensive. The problem, however, revolved not about launch but about recovery.

TOP: **Despite its diminutive size – its span was only 7.8m/25.8ft – and low power, the Sopwith Baby served until July 1917, when it was superseded by the Pup.** ABOVE: **Both British and German fleets explored the possibilities of aircraft working with submarines. Here, in May 1916, the E22 trims down to float off two ramp-mounted Sopwith Schneiders, instantly recognizable from their distinctive bull-nosed engine cowling.**

Radio communication between aircraft and ship had been demonstrated up to a range of 145km/90 miles, but the equipment remained fragile and unreliable.

The introduction of the folding wing by the Short brothers made for more compact stowage aboard ship. However, they were detrimental to a biplane's performance and easily removable wings were also tried.

Recreational flying was already popular before the war, with small seaplanes competing for the Schneider Trophy. Sopwith's design for a Schneider competitor provided the basis for his Tabloid. Even loaded, it weighed only 771kg/1,700lb and pioneered the evolution of launch and recovery routines, particularly in the use of flying-off ramps. Development of a more powerful engine saw the Tabloid evolve into the widely used Baby.

ABOVE: **In order to reduce the landing run of carrier aircraft, some had their wheels experimentally replaced by skids, as on this Pup. Note also the 1918 fore-and-aft arrester wires, raised by a portable wooden ramp.** LEFT: **A Sopwith 1½-Strutter suspended from *Furious*' starboard transfer derrick. As the ship had no usable landing deck, this spectacular damage was caused, presumably, by a drop.**

In contrast, the torpedo-carrying Short 184 appeared enormous, with over twice the wingspan and weighing in at over 3.01 tonnes/3 tons. Equipped with successively uprated engines, about 650 were built by a range of sub-contractors, and they saw service throughout the war.

Sopwith designs predominated for RNAS fighters, with Bristol and Parnall also of note. Introduced late in 1915, Sopwith's 1½-Strutter set a new standard, serving either as a two-seat fighter or as a single-seat bomber.

From early in 1916, the smaller Sopwith Pup complemented the 1½-Strutter. Agile, but with a low landing speed, the Pup served widely with the fleet. In turn, however, it was superseded by the 2F.1 Camel. Slightly larger and more powerful, the Camel had a greater useful payload and two forward-firing machine-guns.

By April 1918, when the RNAS and RFC were amalgamated into a single, unified Royal Air Force (RAF), over 100 aircraft were being carried by cruisers and capital ships, the Sopwith Cuckoo torpedo aircraft was in service and a new, anti-submarine role had been added.

ABOVE: **Out of her element; a Fairey Campania at a Royal Naval Air Station. As the name implies, the aircraft was designed specifically to operate from the ship of that name. Note the four-bladed propeller.**

Typical British shipborne aircraft of World War I

	Wing span	Speed	Power	Machine-guns	Payload
Sopwith Schneider	7.8m/25ft 8in	140kph/87mph	75kW/100hp	1	29.5kg/65lb
Sopwith Baby	7.8m/25ft 8in	161kph/100mph	97kW/130hp	1	59kg/130lb
Short 184	19.4m/63ft 6in	143kph/89mph	194kW/260hp	1	236kg/520lb
Fairey Campania	18.8m/61ft 8in	137kph/85mph	205kW/275hp	1	59kg/130lb
Sopwith 1½-Strutter	10.2m/33ft 6in	164kph/102mph	97kW/130hp	1	118kg/260lb
Sopwith Pup	8.1m/26ft 6in	180kph/112mph	60kW/80hp	1	29.5kg/65lb
Sopwith 2F.1 Camel	8.2m/26ft 11in	200kph/124mph	112kW/150hp	2	45kg/100lb
Sopwith Cuckoo	14.2m/46ft 9in	167kph/104mph	149kW/200hp	0	386kg/850lb

Rigid airships after World War I

For navies other than the German, the large rigid was very much a useful-looking invention that never found an application. Following the failure of its first effort in 1911, the Royal Navy did not begin again until 1914, its technology now well behind that of Germany. The first, R.9, went operational in April 1917 and, between then and 1919, when the Admiralty decided that no more would be built, a total of ten was produced, all considered experimental.

In 1918, R.23 was the first to carry its own defensive fighter aircraft. R.31 and R.32 were built to German Schütte-Lanz principles but the laminated wood frames were heavy and difficult to fabricate. R.33 onwards followed closely the design of the captured Zeppelin L.33, the R.34 making a celebrated first-ever double crossing of the Atlantic in July 1919.

Although a conference of December 1918 minuted that rigids were still considered to be valuable for fleet reconnaissance, the general lack of clarity over manning and responsibility following the establishment of the unified Royal Air Force in the previous April, led the Admiralty to cease further development. Some existing rigids soldiered on through the 1920s but never progressed beyond the experimental stage for military application. The R.101 disaster of October 1930 finished British involvement for good.

American naval aviation may be said to date from October 7, 1913, with the establishment by the Secretary of the Navy of a board to "prepare a comprehensive plan for the organization of a Naval Aeronautic Service". Although an unspecified "fleet

TOP: **The Armstrong Whitworth-built R.33 was a straight copy of the German L.33, which force-landed and was burned-out on the Essex coast. With the Admiralty losing interest in airships in 1919, the craft was transferred to the Air Ministry.** ABOVE: **The control car of the USS *Akron* was a beautiful example of American 1930s streamlined styling.**

dirigible" was listed as a requirement from the outset, resistance by many to "big bags" kept wartime dirigibles to non-rigids.

A more specific requirement of November 1916 nonetheless specified one "experimental Zeppelin" for which the starting point would prove to be the acquisition of the German L.49,

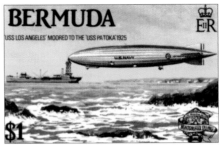

LEFT: **Zeppelin technological know-how was used by Goodyear in the design and construction of the USS *Akron* (seen here) and *Macon*. Giant airship hangars became an architectural form in themselves.**

BERMUDA

'USS LOS ANGELES' MOORED TO THE 'USS PATOKA' 1925

$1

ABOVE: **To explore the possibilities of airship co-operation with the fleet, the US Navy fitted the oiler *Patoka* with basic facilities, including a mooring mast, as depicted on this modern postage stamp.**
BELOW: **Both to extend visual reconnaissance range and for a measure of protection, the *Akron* and *Macon* carried the compact Curtiss F9C/09C Sparrowhawk. Carried within the airship's envelope, the aircraft could be lowered on a trapeze for launch and eventual recovery.**

captured in October 1917. To gain experience a close copy, even down to its Maybach engines, was constructed by the US Navy. Completed as the ZR.1 in 1923, but named USS *Shenandoah*, the craft was something of a disappointment. This was due mainly to her being inflated with helium, a safe gas but not as buoyant as the hazardous hydrogen used by the Germans. Vulnerability to weather was, as ever, the greatest danger and the craft was destroyed in a storm in September 1925 due, it was concluded, to ruptured gas cells.

This was already the US Navy's second such disaster. The epic flight of the British R.34 had resulted in the purchase of R.38, designated ZR.2, in 1921. Still on trials with an Anglo-American crew, she crashed in British waters in August 1921 with the loss of most of those aboard.

Delivered in October 1924, the US Navy's third large rigid was built by the Zeppelin company as war reparation. Officially ZR.3, but named USS *Los Angeles*, she operated successfully until retired in 1932.

ZRS.4 and ZRS.5, USS *Akron* and *Macon* respectively, were built by Goodyear jointly with Zeppelin. Their lives, too, were short. *Akron* was completed in 1931 and lost in April 1933, the *Macon* commissioned in 1933 and was lost in February 1935, both being destroyed in storms at sea.

All three later American rigids could launch and recover their own defensive fighter aircraft but, by the 1930s, they no longer had any military application. With the demolition of the *Los Angeles* in 1939 the large rigid airship, at least as a vehicle of war, passed into history. Feared, misunderstood, over-evaluated, it had proved to be an evolutionary dead-end for naval aviation.

ABOVE: **Based on the late Zeppelin L.49 design, the ill-fated USS *Shenandoah*, here seen moored to the *Patoka*'s mast, was built in the United States. Her buoyancy depended upon helium, giving her an inferior performance.**

The Sempill mission and Japanese naval aviation

At the end of the 19th century, British and Russian interests in the Far East differed sharply. The Russians also had differences with Japan which, having defeated China over Korea in 1894–95, was an up-and-coming regional power. Russia and Japan would themselves go to war in 1904–5 but during 1901, they had begun serious negotiations aimed at rapprochement, a development that caused great concern to the British, who feared an alliance between them.

Despite the size of Britain's late-Victorian navy, its resources were not infinite and many of its ships were far from up to date. Its representation in the Far East could probably have matched that of the Russians but not in combination with the Japanese who, in defeating the Chinese at the Battle of the Yalu, had demonstrated their ability to successfully fight a "modern" naval action.

Thus, with the first signs of Russo-Japanese understanding in 1901, the British made discrete diplomatic moves to pre-empt any formal treaty. The result, signed on January 30, 1902, was an Anglo-Japanese agreement, valid initially for five years. The new alliance agreed, inter alia, that if either were to be

TOP: **Dating from the turn of the century, the *Idzumo* (seen here) and her sister *Iwate* were 9,906-tonne/9,750-ton armoured cruisers from the renowned Elswick yard of Armstrong Whitworth. Following long and useful careers they were destroyed together at Kure by US naval aircraft in July 1945.** ABOVE: **With the virtual annihilation of a Russian squadron at Tsushima in May 1905, Japan became the primary sea power of the western Pacific. In a classic Japanese rendering, a Russian capital ship is overwhelmed by gunfire.**

attacked by a third power, the other would remain neutral. The other would assist if requested only if a fourth power was involved. Thus it was that Britain did not intervene during the Russo-Japanese War of 1904–5, but Japan assisted militarily during World War I.

To Japan's advantage, Britain built her capital ships and trained her personnel to the point where she could proceed independently. In return, the British were content to have a strong Far Eastern ally, allowing the Royal Navy to build up its

RIGHT: **Seen aboard an unidentified carrier, the Nakajima A2N2 of the early 1930s was the first Japanese naval fighter capable of holding its own against any foreign competition. Used extensively against China, it was already obsolescent.**
BELOW: **In order to establish its own naval air arm, the Japanese government sought British assistance. A team of 30 experts, headed by Sir William Forbes-Sempill, here seen second from left, accordingly arrived in Japan in 1921.**

strength in home waters, where the naval race with Germany was gathering momentum. In 1905, both partners were pleased to tighten the terms of the alliance and to renew it for ten years. By this date, however, the United States was viewing Japan as an increasingly unfriendly power, and the new agreement caused considerable disquiet.

In 1914 the Japanese Navy modified the *Wakamiya* similarly to the early Royal Navy seaplane conversions, later adding a flying-off deck forward, in connection with which it acquired Sopwith Pup fighters.

At the close of hostilities the Japanese made a formal request for British assistance in setting up a naval air arm. Well aware of American hostility, Britain agreed, but only on a "semi-official" basis. Consequently, in 1921, a party of 30 experienced officers travelled to Japan under the leadership of Sir William Forbes-Sempill, late Deputy Director of the new Air Ministry (later Baron Sempill).

Japan, although well behind Britain in naval air aviation technique, was at this time little behind the United States. Her first carrier, *Hosho*, was nearly ready to launch and the British quickly trained-up their charges, so that the first deck landing was made in February 1923.

By this time, strong American opposition to the Sempill mission had been largely instrumental in bringing about the abrogation of the Anglo-Japanese Alliance at the Washington Conference, to the deep offence of the Japanese.

ABOVE: **Consequent to the Sempill mission, Japan acquired the designs of several British aircraft. Here Japanese ratings are seen with a licence-built Sopwith Cuckoo, produced by Mitsubishi as the B1M1 (Type 13).**

The Americans, it transpired, had good reason to distrust the mission for, although it was also a commercial success, with British products and designs being acquired, several of its members, including the renowned "Rutland of Jutland", were successfully subverted by their hosts.

The verdict of history is that, while the Japanese would eventually have caught up with American expertise in the field, the British considerably expedited the process.

The Washington Treaties (1921–22)

The British wartime policy of containment resulted in the German battle fleet being neutralized rather than defeated. In the Mediterranean, much the same could be said of the Austro-Hungarian fleet.

Following Jutland, the Germans switched emphasis to the submarine war but although considerably slowed, their capital ship construction programme still proceeded. Yet to be finished were two *Bayern*-class battleships and four *Mackensen*-class battle-cruisers. Already formidable ships, the latter were even more exaggerated by the conflicting and sketchy intelligence reports. Unsurprisingly, therefore, both the British and Americans embarked on new classes of super-dreadnoughts to counter them.

ABOVE: **The limits of 10,160 tonnes/10,000 tons and 203mm/8in guns set for cruisers by the Washington Treaty unintentionally triggered a "cruiser race". The Japanese *Kumano* was one of a long series that cheated on limitations.**

ABOVE: **Built to implement remaining carrier tons, the USS *Wasp* (here seen commencing builder's trials in late 1939) proved to be too small, her operational capability limited by inadequate speed and flight deck dimensions.**

Determined to be the dominant western Pacific sea power, Japan was not to be outdone, commencing her ambitious "8/8" programme. In the Mediterranean, the French and Italians were building as much in competition with each other as in the necessity to counter the largely inactive Austro-Hungarians.

The wartime alliance of the five powers had appeared solid enough, but this solidarity disguised deep divisions, suspicions, and rivalries that surfaced again all too readily once the primary, mutual threat was overcome. Because of these, and for reasons of national pride, a new and ruinously expensive "naval race" was quickly developing. Sensing that public opinion was broadly hostile, the Americans pre-empted a developing British initiative by inviting all five powers to a Conference on Limitation of Armament. This duly opened in Washington on November 12, 1921, and, on their home ground, the Americans were at a distinct advantage, their code breakers eavesdropping on communications between the delegations and their governments.

The powers surprised even themselves with their readiness to consign their new construction programmes and many existing warships to oblivion. It was agreed that Great Britain, the United States, Japan, France and Italy should limit their

LEFT: Special clauses had to be built into the agreement to allow the oversized *Lexington* and *Saratoga* to be converted to aircraft carriers. *Lexington*'s fine entry is shown well here. ABOVE: The treaties allowed carriers to carry guns of up to 203mm/8in in the mistaken belief that they could, and should, be able to fight off cruisers. The *Saratoga*, which survived the war, had these useless appendages removed in favour of a 127mm/5in dual-purpose armament.

global capital ship tonnage to a fixed ratio of 5:5:3:1.75:1.75, the respective maxima being 533,425:533,425:320,055: 177,808:177,808 tonnes or 525,000:525,000:315,000: 175,000:175,000 tons.

Aircraft carriers were also specifically limited. Defined as vessels of at least 10,160 tonnes/10,000 tons displacement, designed for the *specific and exclusive* purpose of carrying aircraft, they were subject to the same ratio of construction. In this case, the overall tonnages should not exceed 137,166: 137,166:82,300:60,963:60,963 tonnes or 135,000:135,000: 81,000:60,000:60,000 tons. Carriers in existence, or building, on November 21, 1921, would be deemed "experimental" and not count against global totals.

No new carrier could exceed 27,433 tonnes/27,000 tons except that two, of up to 33,530 tonnes/33,000 tons, might be converted from hulls that would otherwise be scrapped. Like capital ships, carriers could be replaced only 20 years after their date of completion.

The Japanese came away resentful. They had pressed for a 10:10:7 ratio but had failed, and their valued Anglo-Japanese Alliance had been diluted to a face-saving but ineffective Four-Power Pact. The British had agreed to this only under considerable pressure from the United States, Australia and New Zealand.

> "I am convinced that a war with Japan is about as likely as a war with Mars." Senator Thomas Walsh of Montana. Debate following President Coolidge's address to Congress, December 1923

Concerned that the Japanese had been given mandate of many ex-German, western Pacific island groups, the Americans negotiated a general non-fortification clause, but with specified exceptions.

By agreeing to the aforementioned ratios Great Britain had also agreed to the abandonment of her traditional naval superiority. Since 1915, the US Navy had been pursuing a "second to none" policy and the British now accepted its demands for parity.

Ratified in 1923 and not to be terminated until 1936, the limitations imposed by the Washington Treaties would have a profound effect on the development and design of aircraft carriers in particular.

ABOVE: The first battleships ever to mount 406mm/16in guns, the two Japanese *Nagato*-class survived the severe culls imposed by the Washington Treaties. Surprisingly, neither was sunk by hostile action.

ABOVE: By concentrating the main battery, the designers of the British *Nelsons* were able to work in thicker armour over a limited area in order to comply with treaty limitations.

Carrier operational philosophies

Argus was the 100-eyed messenger of mythology and the name was entirely appropriate for Britain's first true aircraft carrier whose primary roles had been seen as spotting and reconnaissance as well as flying anti-Zeppelin patrols. So fast was naval aviation developing, however, that by the time of the ship's completion in 1918, mass airborne torpedo attack had been added. The objective here was specifically to neutralize a reluctant enemy fleet in its own ports. The attack never materialized because the necessary numbers of flight decks or aircraft were never available.

As it was accepted that capital ships at sea could not be destroyed by the small warheads of air-dropped 457mm/18in torpedoes, the objective was to use the weapon to slow an enemy sufficiently to be finished by gunfire – as would be demonstrated at Matapan and in the sinking of the *Bismarck*.

Thus, throughout the 1920s, the British carrier remained firmly wedded to the battle fleet, providing long-range reconnaissance, fighter air-cover and limited torpedo-bomber capacity. Only in the 1930s, and probably influenced by the Americans, did the Royal Navy start to look at operating carriers as a group, and independently of the battle fleet.

At the close of the Washington Conference in 1922, the British were well ahead in expertise but their ships were eclectic and not of efficient design. Unlike the United States and Japan, Britain had none of her planned super-dreadnoughts under construction and, therefore, was unable to take advantage of the treaty clause that permitted the conversion of two large hulls.

TOP: **Fairey III Fs aboard HMS *Courageous* in the 1930s. Arrester wires were not then in use and these aircraft were not fitted with hooks. Note the "planeguard" destroyer, positioned to assist in the event of a flying accident.** ABOVE: **As, by far, the largest carriers in the world the USS *Lexington* (seen here) and *Saratoga* were able to establish and develop operational philosophies based on large air wings and high ship speeds.**

Flanking the Pacific, the fleets of America and Japan surveyed each other with thinly disguised hostility. With respect to the vast distances involved, each thought in terms of long endurance, with operational time extended by replenishment at sea.

The American Plan Orange was based on a battle fleet with a strong amphibious element advancing steadily through the presumed fortified Japanese-mandated island groups in order to recover lost territories. Land-based aerial opposition could be expected but the principal threat emanated from the Japanese fleet, specifically its carriers.

LEFT: **Seen here in 1930, the *Saratoga* has much of her air wing ranged on deck. Her battle cruiser origins are evident in the fine stern configuration and the enormous casing that was four funnels in one.**
BELOW LEFT: **One of the best-known Fleet Air Arm aircraft between the wars was the Fairey III F. Although its first flight was made in 1926 it was not finally phased out until 1940. It served also as a float-fitted seaplane.**
BELOW: **Within days of Pearl Harbor, Japanese air power again proved its potency when the British capital ships, *Prince of Wales* (seen here leaving Singapore) and *Repulse* were caught without air cover, overwhelmed and sunk off the Malayan peninsula.** BOTTOM: **Seen here being catapulted, the Japanese Kawanishi E7K (Type 94) was widely used for reconnaissance flying from capital ships and cruisers. Known to the Allies as "Alf", it had a very distinctive engine note.**

"[The Japanese aircraft carrier] must be prepared to be impaled as it impales the enemy."
Japanese Staff College study of November, 1936

The two big *Lexingtons* allowed the US Navy to examine the merits of large air wings and how they should be composed, not least to provide fighter cover for the fleet. Not impressed with the average pilot's ability to hit a freely-manoeuvring warship by either level bombing or torpedo, the Americans pioneered the later deadly technique of dive-bombing.

For the Japanese, the American fleet was the primary target. Much of the reconnaissance role was assumed by the float planes carried aboard all major warships, leaving the carriers the maximum capacity for offensive aircraft.

In order to strike first, the Japanese emphasized range as a paramount factor in aircraft specification. The major barrier to the destruction of an American fleet would then be its carriers, which therefore became the primary objective. Their neutralization meant that the Japanese carriers (fewer than the Americans because of the limitations imposed by the Washington Treaties) would be freed from the need to directly support the battle fleet and could operate either alone or in mutually supportive groups. The increased risk implicit in this mode of operation was understood and accepted.

Interestingly, it was generally accepted wisdom that a carrier's aircraft could not sink a battleship, the torpedo warheads being too small and dive-bombers achieving insufficient dive velocity. Yet, at the outset of the Pacific war, the British *Prince of Wales* and *Repulse* were destroyed primarily by air-dropped torpedoes, although this was achieved with land-based aircraft.

"Billy" Mitchell and the US Navy bombing trials

Unlike the British, who amalgamated Army and Navy aviation into a single, unified service in 1918, the Americans kept theirs separate. To avoid overlapping responsibilities and wasteful duplication, a Joint Army and Navy Board on Aeronautics had been formed in June 1919, but this did not prevent much agitation and politicking from those who supported the formation of an independent air force. These were mainly army personnel and none was more vociferous than Brigadier General William "Billy" Mitchell, despite President Harding's ruling before Congress in April 1921, that aviation was "inseparable from either the Army or Navy".

In January 1921, the Secretary of the Navy had announced that various ex-German warships would be expended as targets to evaluate the effectiveness of aerial bombing. In this, the Army was invited to participate, but an immediate Army demand for ship targets to conduct its own trials was turned down by the Navy as superfluous and unnecessary.

For the Navy, the exercise was designed to establish three major points: the ability of aircraft to locate ships in coastal waters; the probability of hitting ships with bombs while under

TOP: **Last of the "pre-Dreadnoughts", HMS *Agamemnon* was demilitarized post-war and converted into a radio-controlled target ship. In this role, she was employed in both bombing and gunnery trials. She was scrapped in 1926.** ABOVE: **William Mitchell's publicly avowed aim was to erase the US Navy's function of the nation's "first line of defence", arrogating the role to an air force independent of either army or navy. He is seen here (right) with fellow Army flier L.J. Maitland (left).**

weigh; and ascertaining the damage that such hits might inflict. It was therefore imperative that observers board the target vessel after each stage in order to note the cumulative damage and to make recommendations for improvement in future designs.

Mitchell's forte was to use exaggeration and innuendo to gain press publicity. To the Navy's anger he had recently published the unsubstantiated claim that aircraft could "destroy or sink any ship in existence today". With such an unscrupulous operator, the Navy should have been forewarned, but exercised no authority over him.

In June 1921, the bombing trials were staged off the Virginia Capes with the ex-German targets all anchored, stationary and unmanned. To warm up, Navy aircraft sank three U-boats without difficulty. The Army fliers then took some 20 minutes to dispose of a destroyer. On July 18, interest grew with the light cruiser *Frankfurt*, which took aircraft of both services six hours to sink, using 113–272kg/250–600lb bombs.

The "star turn" was the battleship *Ostfriesland*. To allow naval observers to assess progressive damage, it was specified that only two 113–136kg/250–300lb bombs could be dropped at a time and that only one 454kg/1,000lb bomb could be dropped between each inspection.

On the first day, the ship suffered superficial damage from only light bombs. With the second day, however, Mitchell played his trump. Ignoring the rules and all Navy attempts to call a halt, he sent in a continuous stream of aircraft. The ship was hit from low level with three out of five 454kg/1,000lb bombs and an unspecified number out of six 907kg/2,000lb bombs. It was the near misses that sank the ship, their concussive strength staving-in her hull plating.

As there had been no assessment, the *Ostfriesland* sinking proved nothing other than the obvious truth that stationary ships, with incomplete watertight integrity and no damage control parties, might easily be sunk. Any Navy attempt to point this out, however, was drowned by the blare of Mitchell trumpeting to the press and to the world in general that he had been right all along. Spectacular pictures, released to the press, easily misled an uninformed public.

Accepting that Mitchell had staged a coup, the Navy gritted its teeth and got down to the necessary task of improving horizontal and torpedo protection in its ships. Mitchell himself escaped official censure but, while strengthening the case for aircraft carriers, failed to prove that for an independent air force.

ABOVE LEFT: **As a Brigadier General, William "Billy" Mitchell, like Trenchard in Great Britain and Douhet in Italy, was firmly committed to the concept of the heavy bomber as arbiter of future wars. The means by which he pursued his aims were, however, less than scrupulous.** ABOVE: **Dating from 1893, the USS *Indiana* (BB.1) was sunk by the US Navy in explosives trials, simulating bombing, on November 1, 1920. Details were leaked to the international press by, it was believed, Mitchell for his own purposes.** BELOW: **Effectively hijacking the Navy's 1921 bombing trials, Mitchell demonstrated that a battleship (the ex-German *Ostfriesland*) could be destroyed by the concussive mining effect of near misses.** BOTTOM: **The ex-German light cruiser *Frankfurt* was expended in the same series of bombing trials as was the *Ostfriesland*. While the sinkings gained extensive publicity, they proved nothing.**

"Day of the battleship ended."
Newspaper headline after the *Ostfriesland* sinking

Catapults and arresters

Not as ready as the British to accept simple, but effective, flying-off platforms, the Americans worked on catapults from an early stage. From 1916, the British trials ship *Slinger* was evaluating two separate patterns while the US Navy had fixed quarterdeck units on several armoured cruisers. Both programmes were fraught with technical problems, although the USS *North Carolina* made a first under-weigh launch on July 12, 1916.

With the introduction of the through flight deck aircraft carrier there was adequate space for the light aircraft of the time to make rolling take-offs and catapults (or "accelerators") were not fitted to HMS *Argus*. Not completed until 1922, the USS *Langley* had a catapult from the outset. Other patterns were also evaluated but all were removed by 1928 as not being much used.

Arrester gear was a different matter. First tried as transverse wires with deadloads when Ely made his pioneer landing on the *Pennsylvania* on January 18, 1911, it reappeared in 1917 in HMS *Furious'* second rebuild. Although her after flying-on deck was to prove virtually unusable, it was fitted with fore-and-aft arrester wires. These, raised slightly from the deck, were designed to engage in hooks protruding from the skids that served her Sopwith Pups in place of wheeled undercarriages. A transverse wire system with deadloads was also tried out,

ABOVE: **A Curtiss Model F, AB-3, gets airborne from the fixed catapult installation on the afterdeck of the armoured cruiser USS *North Carolina* (CA-12) on July 12, 1916.** BELOW: **Catapulted from the British escort carrier HMS *Empress*, a Grumman Avenger torpedo-bomber releases the strop as it gets airborne.**

but so few landings were attempted that meaningful comparisons could never have been made. As a crash barrier, the *Furious* had a transverse frame strung with vertical cables.

Initially with an arrester system, the *Argus* was quickly fitted with a fore-and-aft wire arrangement, mainly to avoid wind gusts sweeping a landing aircraft over the side. Experiments

RIGHT: **Before aircraft land-on, a crew member sets up the barrier aboard an escort carrier of World War II. The torpedo-like object is a paravane streamed to divert mine cables.**

ABOVE: **Despite the longitudinal arrester wires, this skid-fitted Sopwith Pup has still slewed. Note the barriers used for these trials, the one in the foreground to prevent overshooting, the other (together with the handling party) to prevent the aircraft toppling overboard.**

involved the use of paired ramps that served both to elevate the wires and to slow the aircraft. It was soon found necessary to alter the cables so that they could be lowered to the deck to allow aircraft to taxi freely. A further refinement was introduction of a Landing Signals Officer, to indicate to a pilot when he was engaged with the wires and, by extension, to give him alignment on his approach to touch-down.

Fore-and-aft wires were far from satisfactory, not least in tending to cause aircraft to pitch on their noses. From 1925 until 1931, the Royal Navy abandoned them altogether on carriers. After the close of hostilities in 1918, the Americans no longer enjoyed the result of British experience and, in going their own way, benefited by the early adoption of transverse wire systems, retarded with friction brake-drums.

With no brakes and in the absence of wires, a carrier aircraft relied mainly on headwind to come to a halt. Heavier aircraft demanded the reinstatement of arresters as well as the installation of catapults. In the Royal Navy the first carriers so fitted on a permanent basis were the *Courageous* and *Glorious* in 1934. These were able to launch a 3,175kg/7,000lb aircraft at 56 knots. The aircraft themselves were also by now strong enough to withstand the considerable forces involved.

American carriers placed considerable importance on astern speed so that, in an emergency, aircraft could be landed over the bows. This entailed a second set of arrester wires forward. Large air strikes meant "spotting" ready aircraft on deck, and the technique was to catapult aircraft away until such time as there was sufficient free space to allow the remainder to make the slightly faster rolling take-offs.

TOP: **An artificer conducts a pre-launch check on a catapult. Note how the Japanese dolly runs along a raised track, the wheels of the aircraft's undercarriage remaining on the deck.** ABOVE: **How it should be done. The hook of an F6F Hellcat has engaged with the transverse arrester wire which, damped by hydraulic cylinders, has decelerated the aircraft without damage. Note the light construction of the flight deck on wartime American carriers.**

Aircraft aboard submarines

Although by no means "aircraft carriers", submarines of most major fleets have carried aircraft, mainly with a view to extending their limited horizons.

No World War I U-boat appears to have been intended for such a function but, on January 6, 1915, the *U-12* of the Flanders flotilla carried a Friedrichshafen FF-29a floatplane on its casing to a point within range of the English coast. The boat was flooded down to float off the aircraft, which then made a symbolic flight over enemy territory. The risk to boat and crew was considerable, attracting official opprobrium.

This, however, was a time of considerable aviation innovation and several companies – Hansa-Brandenburg, LFG and Heinkel – were moved to build prototypes for use aboard submarines. None entered German service.

After the 1918 armistice, the US Navy acquired German U-boat technology. It was impressed by the big *U-142*-class cruiser submarines, apparently well-suited to Pacific operations. At some stage it appears that a small aircraft had

been considered for these boats and the Americans conducted trials aboard their submarine *S-1*, using a Caspar-Heinkel U-1 floatplane. The results were not encouraging, so plans to incorporate a pressure-tight, topside hangar on the cruiser submarines *V-5* and *V-6* of 1926, were abandoned.

In 1927, the British converted the big minelaying submarine *M2* to carry a specially-built Parnall Peto floatplane. A cylindrical, pressure-tight hangar was built into the forward side of the superstructure, its door opening directly on to the catapult which ran the length of the forward casing. The arrangement was cumbersome, slow in operation and not judged a success. Its complexity and vulnerability probably caused the loss of the boat by foundering in 1932.

The *M2* experiment was quickly taken up by the French who, between 1927 and 1934, built their monster *Surcouf*, for a long time the world's largest submarine. She was large enough to incorporate two 203mm/8in guns into her forward superstructure and, at its after end, a cylindrical hangar for a knocked-down Besson MB.411 "observation seaplane". Although the submarine operated, and was lost, under the Free French flag during World War II, there is no evidence that either aircraft or guns had ever been of significant use.

Ever committed to the deployment of reconnaissance floatplanes from all conceivable platforms, it was the Japanese that most fully exploited the concept of aircraft aboard submarines. Experimentation with a small Heinkel aircraft began as early as 1923. Given folding wings, this design was developed as the Yokosuka E6Y1 and flew from the large minelaying submarine *No.48* in 1927.

When other fleets had dropped the practice, the Japanese persevered. In 1935 they produced the little Watanabe E9W1 ("Slim"), superseded in 1941 by the more capable E14Y1 ("Glen"). These were intended for reconnaissance but, as the war moved against the Japanese, a new, offensive role was explored. During 1944, the first of the I-400 class submarines was completed. These dwarfed even the French *Surcouf* and held the record as world largest until the advent of nuclear power. Their designed function was to attack high-value targets on American soil, using a new, high-performance floatplane, the Aichi M6A1 Seiran. Three of these, plus spares, were accommodated in an enormous cylindrical topside hangar which gave on to a foredeck catapult.

In the event, Japan's desperate straits by 1945 saw the craft used for cargo-carrying. Only two were completed as Seiran carriers, and both of these too late to be of any use.

ABOVE: **For a long time the world's largest submarine, the French *Surcouf* was designed around an observation aircraft and a pair of 203mm/8in guns.**

ABOVE AND BELOW: **During 1923 the US Navy also explored the possibilities of submarines carrying seaplanes. A knock-down Martin MS-1, derived from a wartime German design, was stowed in a pressure-tight canister abaft the conning tower. The facilities were not as elaborate as those of the *M2* but, like the British, the Americans saw little value in the venture and future development was abandoned.**

LEFT: **Probably the ultimate in aircraft-carrying submarines, the Japanese I-400 class of World War II copied the layout of the British *M2* in that the centrally located pressure-tight hangar gave directly on to a foredeck catapult. As three floatplanes could be accommodated, however, the scale was considerably greater.** ABOVE: **An I-400 type in profile with an Aichi M6A1 floatplane on the catapult. Note the crane, which could be folded down into the casing, and the 139.7mm/5.5in gun aft.**

Inter-war development in carrier aircraft

During 1918–39, the undisputed lead in naval aviation enjoyed by the Royal Navy was emphatically lost to the fleets of the Japanese and the United States. Operating philosophies and, later, ship design resulted in too few aircraft aboard each carrier, so each aircraft design was multi-purpose. For navigation purposes, each usually was at least a two-seater, and most had to be interchangeable between floats and wheeled undercarriage, all of which reduced performance. A cash-strapped Royal Air Force, now responsible for the provision of Fleet Air Arm (FAA) aircraft and personnel, could afford only the minimum of either. By 1939, the FAA was back under naval control but damage already done was sufficient to adversely affect the service's performance during World War II.

British carrier aircraft were defined as spotter/reconnaissance, fighter/reconnaissance and torpedo/bomber (later torpedo-dive-bomber). The run of Sopwith fighters was broken in 1923, when the Camel was superseded by the Fairey Flycatcher. The Fairey III F three-seater spotter/reconnaissance aircraft served until replaced by the Hawker Osprey (fighter/reconnaissance) and the Fairey Swordfish (torpedo/spotter/reconnaissance). Only in 1937 did the FAA receive an effective dive-bomber in its first monoplane, the Blackburn Skua. Its poor performance as a fighter, however, saw it replaced largely by the still-ineffective Fairey Fulmar, with eight guns but insufficient speed.

American naval aviation received a tremendous boost in 1926 when the Morrow Board recommended the acquisition of 1,000 aircraft. Unlike in Britain, naval aviation remained fully under naval control. Aircraft were thus not "navalized" land designs but robust machines designed for the hard life aboard a carrier.

The first fighter *was*, however, modified from an existing design but this, the Boeing FB-2, then progressed to be FB-5 before being replaced in 1928 by the F2B. The series continued until 1937 with the F3B and the well-remembered F4B. From

ABOVE: **Converted from a battleship hull and designed with a single hangar, HMS *Eagle* was beamy and moved comfortably, but could manage barely 21 knots on a continuous basis. The aircraft on the hook is a Fairey III F floatplane.**

1935, Grumman effectively took over the stubby F2F and F3F. In 1940 came the first monoplane fighter, the highly effective Grumman F4F (Wildcat), immediately ordered also by Britain and France.

The first torpedo-bomber, the Curtiss CS, was superseded in 1926 by the Martin T3M, then the T4M before the very similar 204kph/127mph Great Lakes TG.2. In 1937 came the first monoplane torpedo-bomber, the 332kph/206mph Douglas TBD Devastator. All of these could also act in the scouting role.

The first purpose-designed dive-bomber, the Great Lakes BG-1, entered service in 1934 and could carry a 454kg/1,000lb bomb. In 1938 came the monoplane Northrop BT, which was refined to the Douglas SBD Dauntless by 1941.

Starting with no experience, the Japanese acquired mainly British designs. The Nakajima A1N1 (Type 3) was thus a Gloster-designed fighter, but was improved by 1930 to the A2N1 (Type 90). Replacements passed successfully through

ABOVE: **Designed as a fighter/dive-bomber, the Blackburn Skua was hopeless in the former role but, in its limited existence in the latter, made history by sinking the German cruiser *Königsberg* in Bergen in April 1940, the first major warship to be destroyed by dive-bombing.**

ABOVE: **Introduced in 1936, the Fairey Swordfish has been dismissed by too many wartime writers as "antiquated". It was, however, an aircraft with very special qualities, proving lethal to surface ship and submarine alike. Particularly, Swordfish are associated with Taranto, Matapan and the *Bismarck* pursuit.**

LEFT: **Properly known as the Curtiss Falcon, a multi-purpose dive-bomber/fighter/observation aircraft, the F8C became firmly associated with the first role, adopting the popular name of Helldiver.**
BELOW: **One of a trend to "tubby" fighters, the Grumman F2F entered carrier service in 1935, but in 1938 was superseded by the slightly enlarged and more powerful F3F. This had departed squadron service by the end of 1941.**

the 352kph/219mph A4N1 (Type 95) to the first monoplane fighter, the Mitsubishi A5M4 (Type 96) "Claude" to the legendary A6M (Type O) "Zeke" or "Zero".

The first dedicated attack bomber was the Mitsubishi B1M1 (Type 13) which could carry a 457mm/18in torpedo or 500kg/1,102lb of bombs at 209kph/130mph. Its 1930 replacement, the B2M1 (Type 89), also a Blackburn design, carried a heavier load but was unreliable. It was superseded in succession by the smaller Yokosuka B3Y1 (Type 92), its derivative, the B4Y1 (Type 96) "Jean" and, by the outbreak of war, the monoplane Nakajima B5N2 (Type 97) "Kate".

As a first dive-bomber, the Japanese licence-built the Heinkel He 66 from 1934 as the Aichi D1A1 (Type 94), refining it to the D1A2 (Type 96) "Susie". The Aichi D3A1 (Type 90) "Val" was the first monoplane dive-bomber, serving well into World War II, but proving vulnerable to American fighters.

ABOVE: **The Japanese became interested in dive-bombing in 1930 and, in 1933, acquired rights to the German Heinkel He 66. This was developed successively as the Aichi D1A1, then the improved D1A2 (seen here). Known to the Allies as "Susie", this rugged dive-bomber saw second line war service.** LEFT: **With echoes of a Fairey III D, the Mitsubishi B1M series was conceived by British designers in Japanese employ.**

Armoured versus "open" construction

With tight limitations on individual and global carrier displacement imposed by the 1921–22 Washington Treaties, hard decisions had to be made with respect to carrier design.

The British took the view that a carrier's aircraft comprised her only offensive asset and, therefore, required the maximum reasonable protection. All aircraft were thus to be accommodated internally, protected above from bombing and, to the side, from shellfire. In the early days, the bombing threat was comparatively slight but, with a carrier still expected to be engaged in opposed reconnaissance, that from cruiser gunfire was real. For purpose-designed ships (as opposed to conversions) this led to an arrangement where the flight deck constituted the main strength deck, the hull being continuously plated up to that level and creating an enclosed "box" hangar.

The Americans and, to a lesser extent, the Japanese were influenced by the sheer size of their initial carrier conversions and the obvious advantages that large air wings would confer in a long-range Pacific war. Deck parks were accepted at an early stage but, to maximize below-deck capacity, an "open" design predominated. In this, the hangar (or lower hangar) deck became the strength deck, the hangar walls and flight deck being a relatively light structure that added little to structural strength. Because of their greater depth, British-style hulls suffered lower stresses and could be made lighter. On the other hand, in order to ship an acceptable number of aircraft, British

ABOVE: **The surprisingly elegant lines of HMS *Ark Royal* (II) are seen to advantage following her launch on April 13, 1937. Still in position is the poppet that supported the bows during launch.** BELOW: **The launch of the USS *Ranger* (CV-4) in February 1933. Her very fine lines are apparent, as are the light flight deck substructure and the apertures for three elevators and two groups of three folding funnels.**

LEFT AND BELOW: **Views of *Illustrious* (left) and *Ark Royal* (below) show several points to advantage. Vertical protection of hangar walls was set inboard to allow for a large number of side apertures to accommodate boats, harbour handling arrangements, etc. The aerial view shows how the British arrangement of armament, although giving good all-round coverage, intrudes into the flight deck area.**

carriers required two hangars. The resulting high freeboard kept the flight deck drier but placed it at a height where its weight, hence thickness, became critical.

British operational doctrine between the wars was expressed in terms of small, six-aircraft formations, for which the carriers were adequate. Elsewhere, full deck-load strikes called for much pre-warming of aircraft engines. This had largely to be conducted below and only an open design could provide the necessary ventilation.

From the early 1930s, the dive-bomber emerged as a major threat to carriers. Level bombing from a considerable height could result in horizontal protection being penetrated by relatively small bombs, but accuracy was low. Dive-bombing was accurate and the lower-level release of the bomb was compensated by its far larger weight.

The need to protect against this weapon had a dramatic effect on British carrier design. The 1937 *Ark Royal* (II) had two hangars, a light splinter-proof flight deck, an armoured lower hangar deck and an air wing of 54 aircraft. The following 1940 *Illustrious* had a flight deck armoured over the extent of the hangar, but only one hangar and an air wing of 36. Their size and displacements were comparable. The lower flight deck of the "armoured" carrier made it wetter, while the heavier elevators made operations slower.

The contemporary American view was that the British approach was too "defensive" and that the price to be paid in aircraft numbers was unacceptable.

Wartime experience duly showed British ships' resistance to both dive-bombing and kamikaze strikes, where American and Japanese carriers succumbed or were disabled by comparatively few hits. Conversely, the latter's carriers, with their large air wings, consistently inflicted far more damage.

There is, of course, no simple answer and, as with most ship design, the answer lies in compromise. Sufficient to say that British fleet carriers designed following war experience (*Ark Royal* (III), *Malta*) did not change in philosophy whereas the American equivalents (*Coral Sea*) did, with a corresponding huge rise in displacement.

> **"[T]he British gave up almost 50 per cent of their aircraft capacity to obtain partial protection of the carrier."**
> **US Navy liaison officer aboard HMS *Formidable*, June 12, 1941**

ABOVE: **As an experiment in small fleet carrier design the USS *Ranger* (CV-4) was not a success and was not repeated. Note the funnel arrangements.**
BELOW: **The great hull of the USS *Midway* (CVB-41) takes shape at Norfolk, Virginia. Larger, and more, aircraft, together with a measure of protection demanded a leap in size compared with the preceding Essex class.**

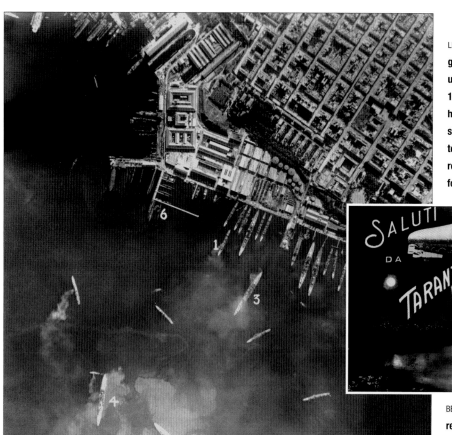

LEFT AND BELOW: **An old postcard invites a visit to the great Italian naval base at Taranto, an invitation taken up by the British Mediterranean Fleet in November 1940. The reconnaissance photography shows clearly how the arsenal fringes the grid of the old town, how ships anchored in the shallow harbour are vulnerable to torpedo attack, and how smaller vessels moored in a row, "Mediterranean fashion", make an excellent target for a bombing pass.**

BELOW: **Completed in 1915, the *Conte di Cavour* was reconstructed to modern standards in 1933–37. Although salvaged following her sinking at Taranto, she required such extensive refurbishment that she saw no further action.**

Taranto

During 1917, the Royal Navy developed plans to hit the German High Seas Fleet in its base with 120 torpedo aircraft. The plan never materialized but the concept survived. In 1938, therefore, with the prospect of war becoming a probability, the British Mediterranean Fleet trained for a moonlight air strike against the Italian fleet in its base at Taranto. In November 1940, the raid took place but on a far more modest scale than envisaged, for the Royal Navy never had sufficient carriers, of which two had already been lost.

Late in the evening of November 11, the new "armoured" carrier *Illustrious* was positioned off the Greek coast, some 274km/170 miles from Taranto. She had a close escort, with distant cover being provided by the Alexandria-based Mediterranean Fleet. The carrier's air group had been reinforced by aircraft from the elderly *Eagle*, temporarily inoperative following a severe shaking by high-level bombing. Even so, the combined strike force comprised just 21 Swordfish biplanes, organized in two waves of 12 and 9 respectively.

> **"Manoeuvre well executed."**
> Signal from C-in-C Mediterranean Fleet to HMS *Illustrious* on her rejoining the fleet the morning after the Taranto raid

Taranto had been under almost hourly surveillance by Malta-based reconnaissance aircraft and, suspecting a reason, the Italians were on high alert. For the raiders, the primary targets were the five battleships reported anchored in the outer harbour, the Mar Grande, protected by anti-torpedo net defences and by barrage balloons. The night selected would silhouette the targets against a three-quarter moon but, in case of overcast weather, the torpedo aircraft would be accompanied by flare-droppers. Further aircraft would provide distraction by dive-bombing ships and facilities in the neighbouring inner harbour, the Mar Piccolo.

In what was known as Operation "Judgement", the *Illustrious* launched her two formations at 20:40 and 21:30 hours. The first achieved surprise but the defences were quickly in action – Italian guns claiming to have fired 13,500 rounds. The cables of the barrage balloons were a considerable hazard to the torpedo aircraft, which came in

LEFT: **Like moths to a flame, *Illustrious*'s Swordfish orbit as they prepare to land-on. Note how flight deck area is maximized by a pronounced overhang at either end.**
ABOVE: **Dating from 1915, the extensively modernized *Caio Duilio* lacked effective sub-division and was put on the bottom by a single 457mm/18in torpedo. She returned to service within a year. The extra elevation of her modernized 320mm/12.6in armament allowed it to outrange the 381mm/15in of equally venerable British battleships.**

> "Twenty aircraft had inflicted more damage upon the Italian fleet than was inflicted upon the German High Sea Fleet in the daylight action at the Battle of Jutland."
> Admiral Cunningham, C-in-C Mediterranean Fleet, writing of the Taranto raid

very low over the outer breakwater, but the open cockpits of the Swordfish and its superb low-speed performance allowed the pilots to see and avoid them in the confused illumination of flares, searchlights and exploding ordnance.

Only about one-third of the planned anti-torpedo netting was actually in place, but this hung to a depth of nearly 10m/33ft, sufficient to protect the battleships from torpedoes fitted with standard contact pistols. However, the British were using newly developed duplex pistols, which would also be actuated by a target's magnetic field if the torpedo were set to run deep, below the target's keel and, by definition, beneath the protective net.

Low speed allowed the well-trained Swordfish aircrews to take their time and to launch accurately. Of eleven torpedoes expended, three hit the battleship *Littorio*, one the *Conte di Cavour* and another the *Caio Duilio*. Surprisingly, considering the small warheads of 457mm/18in torpedoes, all three were put on the bottom. The anchorage was so shallow that none was submerged to much more than upper deck level. All were therefore salvaged, but this operation and subsequent refitting took six months and the *Cavour* saw no further service.

For the loss of just two aircraft, a most economical raid had totally changed the balance of naval power in the Mediterranean at a critical juncture where the French fleet, expected by the British to be a powerful ally, had been immobilized by the unexpected collapse of France and the resulting armistice with the Germans.

ABOVE: **Brand new, the 15-inch battleship *Littorio* succumbed to three 457mm/18in torpedoes. She re-entered service in August 1941. The Italians riposted brilliantly in December 1941, using "human torpedoes" to put the British battleships *Queen Elizabeth* and *Valiant* on the bottom of Alexandria harbour.**

The *Bismarck* operation

One of the earliest functions prescribed by the British Admiralty for the Fleet Air Arm was that of slowing an enemy ship or formation to permit a decision to be reached by a classic gun action. Two such successful examples are afforded by the *Bismarck* episode and the battle of Matapan.

On May 21, 1941, the new German battleship *Bismarck*, accompanied by the heavy cruiser *Prinz Eugen*, sailed from Norway to raid commerce in the North Atlantic. Correctly guessing their intentions, the Admiralty quickly made fleet dispositions to intercept them.

In thick weather, the pair passed north of Iceland but on entering the Denmark Strait (between Iceland and Greenland) late on May 23, they were located by the patrolling cruisers *Norfolk* and *Suffolk*. These tracked and reported their progress southward, enabling British heavy units to intercept them early on the 24th. These, the veteran battle cruiser *Hood* and the brand new battleship *Prince of Wales*, opened fire at 05:53 hours. At 06:00 hours, with the range down to about 12,802m/14,000 yards, the *Hood* was destroyed by a massive explosion. Not yet battleworthy, the *Prince of Wales* broke off the action.

Herself damaged, *Bismarck* signalled her intention to make for a French port. The British cruisers remained in touch, their tracking reports bringing the carrier *Victorious* (also brand new) into range late on the 24th. At 22:00 hours she launched nine

TOP: **HMS *Ark Royal* (II) with one of her Swordfish squadrons. During the *Bismarck* operation, both *Ark Royal* and *Victorious* deployed two Swordfish squadrons. Their admirable low-speed characteristics enabled their carriers to operate them safely in borderline weather conditions.** ABOVE: **The destruction of the battle cruiser HMS *Hood*, unofficial flagship of the Royal Navy, triggered a massive hunt to avenge the loss.**

partially-trained Swordfish, which attacked by radar just after midnight. They obtained one torpedo hit that caused little damage.

The *Bismarck* then made radical changes of course to disguise the detachment of the *Prinz Eugen*. These also caused the cruisers to lose touch. It was now 03:00 hours on the 25th, when Admiral Tovey with the battleship *King George V* and the *Victorious* were barely 161km/100 miles distant.

LEFT: **World War I had adequately demonstrated that sending warships on commerce-raiding cruises was an uneconomic proposition. The loss of the *Bismarck*, not long after that of the *Graf Spee*, proves that some lessons are never learned.** ABOVE: **In the conditions, the *Bismarck* proved to be a difficult target for aerial torpedoes. A single hit at a critical point was, nonetheless, sufficient to slow her and see her brought to battle.** BELOW LEFT: **The pleasing profile of the *Bismarck* was so similar to that of her consort, the heavy cruiser *Prinz Eugen*, that British gunlayers were confused.** BELOW: **Admiral Somerville's Force H, formed around the battle-cruiser *Renown*, the carrier *Ark Royal* (II) and the cruiser *Sheffield* operated with success out of Gibraltar. As such it was able to intervene decisively in the apprehension of the fugitive *Bismarck*.**

Throughout the 25th the British searched blindly, and only at 10:30 hours on the following morning did a patrolling RAF Coastal Command PBY Catalina re-establish contact. The *Bismarck* was under 1,127km/700 miles from Brest and had to be slowed.

Fortunately, the Gibraltar-based Force H had been ordered north and found itself right on the German's projected track. With the group was the carrier *Ark Royal*, whose own aircraft made visual contact by 13:00 hours on the 26th. The cruiser *Sheffield* was detached to sight her and continue tracking.

In a full gale and low, thick overcast weather, *Ark Royal* despatched 14 Swordfish at 14:50 hours. An hour later these attacked blind by radar, only to discover that their target, mistakenly, was the *Sheffield*, then 32km/20 miles from the *Bismarck*. By dint of skilful manoeuvring, the cruiser survived.

It was not until 19:10 hours that a second strike, of 15 Swordfish, could be launched. In truly appalling weather conditions they commenced their attack at 20:47 hours, scoring two hits. One damaged *Bismarck*'s steering and a propeller shaft. Slowed and with her manoeuvrability impaired, she was now doomed.

Throughout the night of the 26th–27th British destroyers worried at her but were unable to inflict further torpedo damage. Before daybreak, however, Admiral Tovey arrived with the battleships *King George V* and *Rodney*. Waiting until full

daylight, Tovey divided his ships and pounded the *Bismarck* to a wreck. Refusing to sink, she was despatched by a cruiser's torpedoes.

The *Hood* had been avenged but it had taken the combined efforts of seven battleships, two aircraft carriers and twelve cruisers to bring the *Bismarck* to book, and then only by virtue of a single aircraft torpedo.

The Battle of Matapan

During March 1941, the British intervention in Greece generated a succession of convoys from the south and, following sustained pressure from their German allies, the Italians despatched a battle group. Sailing on March 26, Admiral Iachino wore his flag in the battleship *Vittorio Veneto* that headed towards eastern Crete in a loose formation, which included 6 heavy cruisers, 2 light cruisers and 13 destroyers.

Aware of the enemy foray, the C-in-C Mediterranean Fleet, Admiral Cunningham, temporarily suspended all convoy movements and sailed late on the 27th with his three veteran battleships, the aircraft carrier *Formidable* and nine destroyers. Already at sea near Crete were his "light forces", four light cruisers and four destroyers. These were ordered to rendezvous with Cunningham late on the 28th but at 06:30 hours that day, they were sighted by the *Veneto*'s catapulted search aircraft. Assuming this to be an isolated group, Iachino decided to engage.

At about 08:00 hours a reconnaissance aircraft from the *Formidable* was reporting the scattered elements of the Italian force at about the same time as three of its heavy cruisers established visual contact with the British light forces. These, outranged, went about and headed south-eastward at maximum speed to draw the enemy on to Cunningham's main body.

Suspicious, the Italians broke off and headed off westward. The British light cruisers complied, only to find that they had been lured on to the *Veneto*.

TOP: **The *Vittorio Veneto*, Italian flagship at Matapan. Although badly damaged by a Swordfish torpedo, she was not sufficiently slowed to allow the veteran British battleships to make an interception.**
ABOVE: **A later British air strike missed the *Veneto*, the primary target, but hit and stopped the heavy cruiser *Pola*. This brought about the battle of Matapan.**

The Italian flagship opened fire at 10:56 hours and, now under 381mm/15in shellfire, the British made a contact report and again fell back. Fortuitously, at this point six *Formidable* Swordfish made a first attack on the *Veneto*. It was unsuccessful but persuaded the Italian admiral to abandon his operation. At 11:30 hours, therefore, he too ceased fire and turned westward for home.

The far slower British battle group, some 105km/65 miles astern but apparently unsuspected, appeared unlikely to be able to intercept Iachino. Then, at 15:20 hours, five more Swordfish from the *Formidable*, supported by high-level RAF bombers from Crete, put a torpedo into the *Veneto*'s port quarter. Still about 644km/400 miles from Taranto, the battleship slowed to 10, then 15 knots.

LEFT: **Sister ship to the *Illustrious*, the *Formidable* flew the critical air strikes that brought about the battle. Like the *Illustrious*, the *Formidable* also survived a later ordeal by dive-bombing that would have destroyed lesser ships.** BELOW: **The widely separated funnels of the Italian cruiser *Pola* show that her machinery spaces were likewise separated. However, a single 457mm/ 18in torpedo was sufficient to bring her to a halt.**

Further air attacks from Crete inflicted no further damage on the enemy but, by 19:00 hours, Cunningham had closed to about 72km/45 miles. To protect the flag the whole Italian force was now tightly grouped and steaming in five columns. Between them, they put up a concentrated barrage of fire when, between 19:35 and 19:45 hours, eight *Formidable* and two Crete-based Swordfish attacked out of the failing light. Only one torpedo found a target, bringing the heavy cruiser *Pola* to a complete halt.

Not appreciating Cunningham's proximity, Iachino pressed on but directed the *Pola*'s two divisional colleagues, *Zara* and *Fiume*, together with four destroyers, to stand by her.

Formidable's aircraft had wrongly claimed to have again hit the *Veneto* so when, at 20:30 hours, the light cruiser *Ajax* reported a radar contact on a stationary ship, Cunningham assumed that it was the Italian flagship which, in reality, was 80km/50 miles further on and making 19 knots.

At 22:30 hours, assisted by radar, the British battleships were just 2,743m/3,000 yards from the preoccupied Italians. Instantaneously, searchlights snapped on and heavy salvoes crashed into the *Zara* and *Fiume* which, with their guns still trained fore-and-aft, were converted in to blazing wrecks. Accompanying destroyers finished off the still-immobile *Pola* and two Italian destroyers.

Although Cunningham was unhappy at the *Veneto*'s escape, what came to be known as the Battle of Matapan established a moral ascendancy that the Italians were increasingly reluctant to challenge. Their fleet remained a powerful threat, but suffered from a deficiency in bold leadership.

ABOVE: **A training session aboard a British escort carrier. The warrant officer and pilot discuss the arming of the torpedo below the Swordfish while crew lie awaiting the order to remove chocks. Note the American-style decking and helmets.** BELOW: **Commander-in-Chief, Mediterranean Fleet at the time of Matapan, Sir Andrew Cunningham is seen here, as Admiral of the Fleet, inspecting the crew of a cruiser. Note the torpedo tubes on the left.**

Pearl Harbor

Aware that any war with the United States would be decided principally on the question of sea control, the Japanese decided to make a pre-emptive strike on the US Pacific Fleet at its forward base of Pearl Harbor. Located on the small Hawaiian island of Oaho, the base was effectively immune to attack except from the air.

All six available Japanese fleet carriers were unobtrusively assembled at a remote anchorage before departing with their escort on November 26, 1941. Having crossed 5,633km/3,500 miles of the lonely north Pacific, the force commanded by Vice Admiral Nagumo Chuichi arrived at its launch point, 443km/275 miles north of its objective, at 06:00 hours on December 7. A first strike of 40 torpedo-bombers, 49 high-level bombers, 51 dive-bombers and 43 fighters was immediately despatched.

Oahu is irregular and mountainous, with Pearl Harbor on its south coast. The first wave approached down the western side, some of its number peeling away to suppress potential interference from the several military airfields.

> "[A]n unwarranted feeling of immunity from attack... seems to have pervaded all ranks at Pearl Harbor, both Army and Navy."
> Admiral Ernest J. King, Chief of Naval Operations to
> Naval Court of Inquiry, November 6, 1944

TOP: **Destroyed by explosion, the wreck of the battleship *Arizona* burns at her berth in Pearl Harbor. Searing images such as this galvanized the United States from its isolationist detachment.** ABOVE: **Standard torpedo-bomber with the Japanese carrier force, a Nakajima B5N2, Type 97 "Kate" leaves the deck of the *Shokaku*. Its torpedo was specially adapted to function in the shallow waters of the American base.**

The island had been well reconnoitred, the plan well rehearsed. It being a Sunday morning, the bulk of the fleet was alongside for the weekend. To the approaching enemy the view was as had been expected, the anchorage dominated by the line of seven battleships, berthed in pairs. There had been no formal declaration of war and surprise was absolute. In the absence of opposition, the aircraft arrived at 07:55 hours and were able to select their targets with deadly precision.

Armour-piercing bombs, fashioned from heavy naval projectiles, drilled through the battleships' horizontal protection, all but one being hit. Specially developed, shallow-running torpedoes lanced the calm harbour waters to devastate all five capital ships on the outer berth. Only rudimentary anti-aircraft armaments were mounted at this time, and return fire was uncoordinated. At each of the airfields and naval air stations aircraft, parked neatly in rows, were wrecked by bombing and low-level strafing.

At shortly before 09:00 hours the first strike was pulling out as the second arrived, having skirted the island's eastern side. Comprising 54 high-level bombers, 81 dive-bombers and

ABOVE: **Dry dock No.1 at Pearl Harbor after the attack. The battleship** *Pennsylvania* **was only lightly damaged but, in the foreground, the destroyer** *Downes* **is sitting on the blocks, flooded, while the destroyer** *Cassin* **has toppled. The smoke is from a distant fire.**

ABOVE: **Smoke from burning ships forms a backdrop to the devastation at Naval Air Station, Ford Island. An undamaged PBY Catalina patrol amphibian is parked at left.** LEFT: **Architect of the attack was Admiral Yamamoto Isoroku. An intelligent and gifted leader, he undertook the task only with the gravest of misgivings. He knew that Japan could sustain only a short war.** BELOW: **"Battleship Row" under attack. From left to right:** *Nevada*, *Vestal* **outboard of** *Arizona*, *West Virginia* **outboard of** *Tennessee*, *Maryland* **outboard of** *Oklahoma*, **and** *Neosho*.

36 fighters, this force again hit the already stricken "Battleship Row" and the dockyard. The airfields took a further working-over and few American aircraft were able to get airborne.

By 09:45 hours the attack was over. With losses of only 29 of their number, Nagumo's jubilant pilots were returned, still unopposed, to their waiting carriers. They left behind 18 sunken ships, 4 of them battleships. The US Navy had lost 92 aircraft, the Army 96 and over 2,300 servicemen were dead.

The attack on Pearl Harbor was universally condemned as an act of treachery yet, whatever the ethics of the Japanese action, it is undeniable that as a military coup the attack was boldly conceived and efficiently executed. However, it was not a total success. The battleships were elderly yet still commanded too much respect at a point when it was apparent to many that the aircraft carrier had already assumed capital ship status. The enemy's concentration on the battleships resulted in most of the dockyard facilities and oil storage area being left unscathed. By the removal, albeit temporarily, of the battleships from the order of battle, the US Navy was obliged to accept its carriers as more relevant to its interests than the battle line.

Most significantly, Nagumo had struck on a day when no American carriers were in port. They survived through being at sea and would eventually prove to be his nemesis.

The Doolittle Raid and the Battle of the Coral Sea

Carriers had inflicted the pain on Pearl Harbor and it was by carriers that the United States responded. Sixteen Army B-25 Mitchell bombers, led by Lt Col James H. Doolittle, were transported across the Pacific on the *Hornet*'s flight deck and on April 18, 1942, were launched at long range. Hitting Tokyo and three other cities, they flew on to Chinese airfields. Immortalized as "Thirty Seconds over Tokyo", the raid caused only symbolic damage but huge embarrassment to the Japanese authorities. It also served notice that their home soil was no longer beyond reach.

The southward Japanese advance continued, meanwhile, with the despatch of an invasion convoy, bent on doubling the "tail" of New Guinea to take Port Moresby, thereby directly threatening Australia. Forewarned by code breakers, however, the Americans had despatched Rear Admiral Jack Fletcher with the carriers *Yorktown* and *Lexington*.

As a preliminary move, the Japanese made unopposed landings on Tulagi and Guadalcanal in the Solomons. Hitherto unsuspected, Fletcher broke his cover on May 3, 1942, by an ineffective air strike against Tulagi. Approaching to cover the

invasion force were the two large Japanese carriers *Shokaku* and *Zuikaku* whose commander, Vice Admiral Takagi Takao, now knew of Fletcher's presence.

A belt of heavy frontal cloud lay over the area on May 6, beneath which three separate groups manoeuvred, searching. Early on May 7, Japanese search aircraft located the American oiler and her escorts. Wrongly reporting her as a carrier, they caused Takagi to waste a full and massive air strike in their destruction.

Fletcher, not far distant, had meanwhile located the Port Moresby invasion convoy. This, accompanied by the small carrier *Shoho*, was so over-reported that it was assumed to be Takagi's main force. A maximum air strike duly despatched the *Shoho*, the first carrier casualty of the Pacific war.

LEFT: **Heavy with maximum fuel and a token bomb load, a B-25 leaves the *Hornet's* deck. Special guidelines, painted well to the port side, ensure that the bombers' wingtips miss the island.**

ABOVE: **An escort's view as *Hornet* launches her B-25s. The operation brought together Halsey in the *Enterprise* and Mitscher in the *Hornet*, two men who were to dominate the American carrier operations.**

"From Shangri-La."
President Roosevelt's response to reporters demanding
to know from where Doolittle's aircraft had flown to bomb Tokyo

Both admirals were now aware that neither had discovered his major opponent, both of whom had about 120 aircraft. Daylight on May 8, found Fletcher in clear weather, whereas Takagi was still under low cloud. Nevertheless, by 08:30 hours, each had located the other and, in short time, 90 Japanese and 84 American aircraft were airborne.

Yorktown's torpedo aircraft enjoyed no luck but her dive-bombers hit the *Shokaku* twice, leaving her unable to launch aircraft. Many of the *Lexington*'s aircraft failed to find their objective but one further bomb hit was made on the *Shokaku*.

In return, the Japanese torpedo aircraft attacked *Lexington* simultaneously from either bow. Unable to avoid all the torpedoes, she was hit by two of them. Two bomb strikes added to her problems but, within the hour, her damage control teams appeared to be winning just as the ship was wracked by an explosion caused by aviation fuel vapour. It was the first in a devastating series that finally caused her destruction. The *Yorktown* had also been hit by a single heavy bomb.

The Battle of the Coral Sea was significant in that it was the first fought by carrier groups seeking each other's destruction without ever coming within sight of each other (this action was fought at a range of about 322km/200 miles). In material terms, the Japanese came off better in having destroyed the much heavier US carrier, even though the damaged *Shokaku* had to withdraw for major repair. Strategically, however, the Americans won as, with the destruction of the *Shoho*, the invasion convoy turned back. Port Moresby was never to be taken and the mountainous tail of New Guinea would mark the southern limit of what had appeared to be an unstoppable Japanese advance.

TOP: **Dauntless SBD scout/dive-bombers ranged on the *Yorktown*. They were instrumental in the destruction of the Japanese carrier *Shoho* at the Coral Sea, the first carrier loss of the Pacific War.** ABOVE: **The major loss of the Coral Sea action was the American carrier *Lexington*. Severely hit by Japanese torpedo aircraft, she suffered further from dive-bombers. She was destroyed finally by massive internal explosions.**

The Battle of Midway

The Japanese wished to provoke a decisive battle with the US Pacific Fleet before it gained in strength. Their plan was to seize Midway Island, west of Pearl Harbor but close enough to be a threat. On coming to its defence the Americans would be ambushed by Admiral Yamamoto Isoroku and the main Japanese battle fleet. A brilliant leader, Yamamoto had a weakness for very complex plans, that for Midway dissipated his otherwise overwhelming strength.

American intelligence was, however, extraordinarily detailed, enabling the Pearl Harbor-based Admiral Chester Nimitz, C-in-C Pacific to make counter-dispositions in good time, deploying his smaller forces to the best advantage. Once again, carrier groups would be both spearhead and major target. Lacking the two damaged at the Coral Sea action, Vice Admiral Nagumo would use his remaining four carriers to soften-up the defences prior to the assault landing. For the Americans, the *Yorktown*, another Coral Sea casualty, was rapidly patched up and joined by the *Enterprise* and *Hornet*, commanded by Rear Admiral Raymond A. Spruance.

At first light on June 4, 1942, Midway radar detected an incoming strike of over 100 aircraft, half of Nagumo's strength. In a fierce air battle, defending fighters prevented major damage to installations, obliging Nagumo to prepare for an unscheduled second raid. His force had already been located by Midway reconnaissance and was subject to sporadic but ineffective attack by island-based aircraft.

The attack aircraft held back by Nagumo had been fully armed with torpedo and armour-piercing bombs to meet a hoped-for intervention by the American navy. Now there was a requirement for a second strike against Midway and the machines were being rearmed with light-explosive bombs.

ABOVE: **SBD Dauntless dive-bombers ranged aboard the *Enterprise* at Midway. Two squadrons of these were carried, together with one of F4F Wildcat fighters and one of TBD Devastator torpedo-bombers.**

At this juncture, Japanese reconnaissance reported American warships to the north of the island. They might, it indicated, include a carrier. There were, in fact, three and they were about to launch their own strike against Nagumo's force.

Following anxious deliberation, the Japanese admiral decided that the warships had to be the priority target. Once again, his armourers unloaded bombs to rearm the aircraft with torpedoes. Below, ordnance unavoidably littered the hangars while, topside, the flight decks were cleared for the imminent return of the Midway strike.

LEFT: **Working with strong intelligence regarding Japanese intentions, Pearl Harbor-based Admiral Nimitz was able to ignore enemy feint movements and concentrate his forces to maximum advantage.**

ABOVE: **Bombed, torpedoed and listing badly, the *Yorktown* was abandoned. A day later, however, she was still afloat (as seen here with the destroyer *Gwin* standing by). Taken in tow, she fell victim finally to submarine torpedoes.**

"I felt bitter. I felt like swearing."
Admiral Nagumo's Chief of Staff on losing four carriers
at Midway, June 1942

At this vulnerable point the American air strike arrived, its formations somewhat scattered. The torpedo-bombers suffered severe loss but their attack, although without result, drew down Nagumo's top cover. This left the following dive-bombers virtually unopposed and, within minutes, three Japanese carriers were fatally damaged.

The fourth ship of Nagumo's force, the *Hiryu*, put up her own dive-bomber force that followed the bearing taken by the jubilant, returning American fliers. This led it directly to the *Yorktown* which, in turn, was totally disabled by three bomb hits. (Still immobile, she was later despatched by two submarine torpedoes.) *Yorktown*'s search aircraft had, however, already located the *Hiryu*, which was then destroyed by a dive-bomber force from the *Enterprise*.

Spruance remained in the area, his aircraft sinking the heavy cruiser *Mikuma* of the invasion force on June 6. He wisely held back, however, as the dispirited Yamamoto decided to abandon his operation.

The Japanese had suffered a major defeat despite the near presence of a substantial battle fleet that was powerless to change the course of the action. With Nagumo's group had been lost over 100 carrier-trained aircrew, continuing the haemorrhage of experienced personnel which the Japanese were never able to correct and which, ultimately, was to prove decisive.

ABOVE: **Nagumo's flagship *Akagi* is here seen manoeuvring violently to frustrate air attack. It availed her little for, in the words of her Flag Captain "we were unable to avoid the dive-bombers because we were so occupied in avoiding the torpedo attacks".** BELOW: **Disintegrating following a 127mm/5in hit from the *Yorktown*, a Nakajima B5N2 "Kate" sears a fiery trail to mark her passage. Note the torpedo falling away.** BOTTOM: **One of three Japanese bomb hits on the *Yorktown* exploded in the funnel, with the spectacular result shown here. It eventually made the island untenable and brought the ship to a standstill. Note the "not under control" balls.**

ABOVE: **The British escort carrier** *Chaser*, **seen from a catapulted Swordfish. Her mercantile origins are very evident in the hull and post-war, she was reconverted to a Dutch-flag general cargo ship. Note how the island is totally outboard of the flight deck edge.** LEFT: **Seen on her delivery voyage, the American CVE** *Kwajalein* **is carrying a deck-load of some seventy F4U Corsairs to Espiritu Santo in July 1944. All her short life was devoted to ferrying replacement aircraft.** BOTTOM: **An essential component to the US Navy's success in the Pacific was its adequate and highly efficient logistics service. Background to this scene of activity is the CVE** *Casablanca*, **name ship of a 50-strong class that was completed in under one year.**

Escort carriers

Following the fall of continental Europe in 1940, Great Britain's very survival depended upon transatlantic convoys. By 1943, with Germany increasingly fighting on the back foot, the convoys were equally vital to the military build-up prior to the necessary invasion of Europe.

Throughout, the major threat to the convoys was the U-boat while, in the initial stages at least, British and Allied escorts were too few, their speed and endurance being too low. Fortunately, the workhorse of the German submarine service, the Type VII, although continuously improved, had a poor submerged performance, typically 1,287km/800 miles at four knots. It was sufficient, therefore, for an escort to keep a submarine submerged until her convoy had passed, for the submarine could not catch up again unless she hazarded herself by surfacing. The answer was a single patrol aircraft that could force down all U-boats in the convoy's vicinity.

Auxiliary to the U-boat was the Luftwaffe's long-range maritime aircraft, initially the Focke-Wulf Condor, which acquired a Zeppelin-like reputation for circling a convoy

beyond gun range, transmitting its position, course, and speed to marauding submarines. As with the Zeppelin, the antidote was the high-performance fighter. History, having repeated itself, demanded a similar solution, aircraft carriers. Fleet carriers were too few and too valuable to be so employed except for specific operations, so the auxiliary carrier (officially "escort carriers" from August 1942) was reborn.

Both American and British navies had pre-war plans to convert specific large merchant vessels to auxiliary carriers (few of them were, in fact, so converted) but it was only when faced with the realities of convoy warfare in 1940 that both fleets produced prototype escort carriers based on freighter-type hulls of, typically, only 7,000 gross registered tons. Small though their flight decks were and meagre or non-existent their facilities, they could deploy Swordfish ASW and/or Martlet (F4F Wildcat) fighter aircraft. For suppression of U-boats or Condors they were immediately effective.

British yards concentrated on ship repair, so escort carriers (CVE) were series-built in dedicated American construction facilities. Successive classes grew in size and capability, the larger types being retained by the US Navy for the Pacific war. For convoy escort, those under the White Ensign increasingly deployed the F6F Hellcat and the TBF/TBM Avenger, the latter very effective in ASW, carrying bombs, depth charges and rocket projectiles.

Before the arrival of the CVE, U-boats in the so-called mid-Atlantic air gap were untroubled from the air except by the all-too-few specialist VLR (very long range) aircraft, typically Liberators of RAF Coastal Command. The escort carrier, however, could maintain near-continuous, radar-equipped air patrols, denying U-boats the freedom to work around a convoy on the surface, and effectively defeating their integrated "wolf-pack" tactics.

With increasing numbers, CVEs could be spared to form the core of dedicated hunter-killer groups. Armed with Ultra-based intelligence, these especially targeted the enemy's resupply submarines, used to extend the patrols of longer-range operational U-boats.

During the North African landings, at Salerno and, increasingly, in the Pacific, escort carriers took on the task of providing air cover during the assault, followed by close air support for those ashore. The main drawback to their effectiveness in these roles was their limited speed and, in windless conditions, particularly in the tropics, attrition in high-performance aircraft could be considerable. CVEs were also used widely in the endless task of ferrying replacement aircraft.

ABOVE: **Vast wartime programmes resulted in huge numbers of redundant warships post-war. Here, lines of nearly new escort carriers lay in Boston Naval Shipyard in April 1946 awaiting disposal. The nearest, CVE-67, was earmarked for transfer to the Royal Navy but, instead, entered service as the *Solomons*.**

ABOVE: **Until early 1944, F4F Wildcats in Fleet Air Arm service were known as Martlets. Over 300 of these aircraft were acquired for the Royal Navy, giving its carriers a fighter at last equal to the enemy's shore-based machines.** LEFT: **By the close of the European war, the German fleet was largely neutralized. British fleet and escort carriers were thus increasingly able to target essential enemy seaborne supplies. Here, just days before the close of hostilities, aircraft from the CVEs *Queen*, *Searcher* and *Trumpeter* attack shipping near Narvik.**

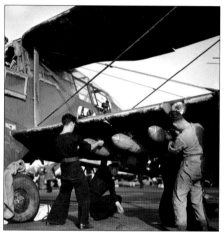

LEFT: **Grumman Avengers on British service. Although designed to carry a 533mm/21in torpedo internally, the aircraft was more often employed by the Royal Navy in a bomber or anti-submarine role, carrying depth charges, bombs or rockets.**
BELOW AND BOTTOM: **Entering service in 1940, the Fairey Albacore was a logical refinement of the Swordfish, which it complemented rather than replaced. In flight, the Albacore showed a much less angular appearance than the Swordfish. Both could carry a 680kg/1,500lb bomb load, shown here as six 113kg/250lb bombs.**

Carrier aircraft development during World War II

British-designed Fleet Air Arm (FAA) aircraft continued to be hedged by requirements for multi-purpose capability, for at least two seats and for very low stall speeds. Fortunately, therefore, the existing and hopeless Blackburn Roc fighter was quickly superseded by the American-sourced Grumman F4F Wildcat. Serving as the Martlet it could, along with the shorter-ranged Seafire and Sea Hurricane, take on high performance enemy land-based fighters and bombers. The F4F, like its successor, the F6F Hellcat, was a dedicated fighter, not encumbered with a secondary function. From mid-1943, the magnificent Chance-Vought F4U Corsair was acquired to work in parallel as a fighter-bomber.

Contemporary two-seat fighter-reconnaissance aircraft were the Fairey Fulmar, then the Firefly. Attempts to utilize more powerful engines in a fighter/torpedo aircraft met failure in the Blackburn Firebrand.

Oft derided, but much respected, the Fairey Swordfish served throughout as a reconnaissance/torpedo aircraft and even, in the absence of fighters, as a dive-bomber. Its successor, the Albacore, was only ever regarded as a less-draughty alternative. From early 1943, the Fairey Barracuda was the FAA's choice dive/torpedo-bomber, serving alongside the excellent Grumman TBF/TBM Avenger, a combination ASW aircraft and torpedo-bomber.

For the US Navy, the single-role F4F and F6F were produced in what, by British standards, were prodigious numbers. With the large *Midway*-class carriers under

construction, Grumman progressed to the twin-engined F7F Tigercat. Essentially a fighter-bomber, valuable in ground support, it entered service only in 1944 and would soon be displaced by jet aircraft.

Later than the Royal Navy, the Americans recognized the merits of the F4U Corsair, yet even these were surpassed by the remarkable Douglas AD-1 Skyraider, which entered service too late to make an impact on World War II.

Until 1943 the standard dive-bomber was the Douglas SBD Dauntless, it being superseded by the Curtiss SB2C Helldiver, capable of carrying a bomb load of up to 1,361kg/3,000lb.

The Japanese began the war with excellent aircraft of all three major categories. Although good performers, however, they had been designed close to their limits and were not

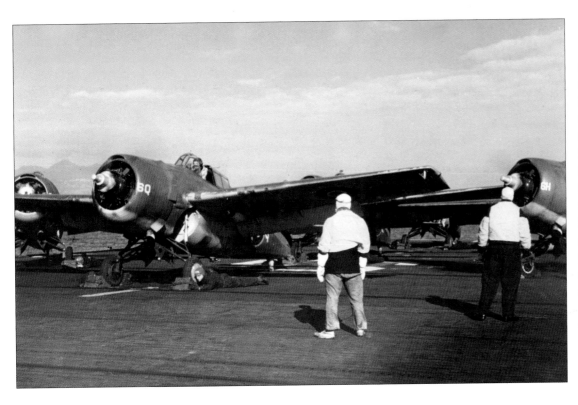

LEFT: **In Royal Naval service the Martlet/ Wildcat was associated mainly with escort carriers where, despite the increasing availability of Hellcats after 1943, it served until the end of hostilities. Robust and reliable, it flew well and, in its six 12.7mm/0.5in machine-guns, packed an adequate punch. Note that deck crew were by now being colour-coded, flight decks being extremely noisy places.**

amenable to further improvement. Under war conditions their successors were too long in development and problem-prone in service, a situation exacerbated by the deteriorating quality of aircrew training.

Introduced in mid-1940, the standard naval fighter was the Mitsubishi A6M (Type O), known as the "Zeke", or "Zero". A light armament, no armour and a fragile airframe were here combined with good aerodynamics to produce a low-level fighter of superb manoeuvrability and exceptional range. It eventually met its match in the F6F, and its successor, the Mitsubishi J2M Raiden, came too late to be of use.

Also introduced in 1940, the Nakajima B5N2 (Type 97) "Kate" proved to be an excellent torpedo-bomber, directly

derived from the B5N1. Again, however, its time in service saw it become ever more vulnerable to defences. Its eventual successor, the B6N Tenzan, proved to have only marginally better performance.

Last of the carrier trio, the Aichi D3A1 (Type 99) "Val" was a satisfactory dive-bomber which, in time, proved deficient in both speed and armament. Its intended replacement, the Yokosuka D4Y1 Suisei, proved to be the fastest carrier-based dive-bomber but was subject to continual technical problems and was difficult for poorly trained pilots to handle.

Ultimately, the Americans prevailed with greater numbers, better organization, and superior design. As importantly, they had plentiful and well-trained aircrew.

LEFT: **Introduced in 1943 as a replacement for the Douglas SBD Dauntless, the Curtiss SB2C Helldiver could deliver three 454kg/1,000lb bombs. Despite the amount of glazing, the crew comprised only pilot and observer/rear gunner.**
ABOVE: **Light and manoeuvrable, the Mitsubishi A6M "Zeke" was deadly in a one-on-one, low-level dogfight. It remained in service too long, however, and was defeated by American second-generation fighters employing manoeuvres and formations based on experience.**

The Battle of Santa Cruz

By October 1942, the island of Guadalcanal marked the southern limit of the Japanese advance. It was being bitterly contested, but the Americans held the initiative with their possession of the only airstrip, Henderson Field. The Japanese army was ordered to storm and take the airstrip on October 25, whereupon the Japanese fleet would close to facilitate the island's capture and, it was hoped, to engage the American carrier force that was providing deep cover.

Early on October 26, a shore-based PBY Catalina located and reported the waiting carrier *Zuikaku*, some 322km/ 200 miles north-west of the Santa Cruz islands. About the same distance to the south-east was Rear Admiral Thomas C. Kinkaid with the American carriers *Enterprise* and *Hornet*. At 05:00 hours these launched 16 dive-bombers on an armed reconnaissance and these, at 06:50 hours, found the smaller enemy carrier *Zuiho*. She, together with the *Shokaku* and *Zuikaku*, were operating in company, once again under the experienced Admiral Nagumo.

At 07:40 hours, two 227kg/500lb bombs wrecked the *Zuiho*'s flight deck, but she had already launched her contribution to Nagumo's opening strike of 65 aircraft. One of his reconnaissance aircraft had located Kinkaid at about 06:30 hours and the strike was away inside 40 minutes. A second strike, of 44 aircraft, was immediately prepared as back-up, using the two larger carriers.

TOP: **The *Enterprise* with two of her SBDs. Although the dive-bombers badly damaged two enemy carriers at Santa Cruz, the ships survived.** ABOVE: **Under attack from dive-bombers and torpedo-bombers, simultaneously, the *Hornet* fights for her life.**

Between 07:30 and 08:15 hours the *Enterprise* sent away 29 aircraft, the *Hornet* 44, which flew in three groups. En route, they encountered the Nagumo strike, both losing aircraft to the escorting fighters.

Awaiting the onslaught, both of Kinkaid's carriers had their escorts close in a tight, protective ring in order to concentrate defensive fire. Overhead were 38 F4Fs of the combat air patrol (CAP). This was poorly directed, and failed to intercept the first enemy wave at a safe range.

ABOVE: The *Enterprise* (seen here) and the *Saratoga* were the only two pre-war American fleet carriers to survive hostilities. LEFT: Wreathed in the smoke from her own anti-aircraft weapons, the battleship *South Dakota* manoeuvres to avoid the attentions of enemy torpedo aircraft while covering the carrier *Enterprise*. BELOW LEFT: An American heavy cruiser, probably *Northampton*, threatened by a low-flying "Kate", whose torpedo is clearly visible.

ABOVE: Deck crews on the *Enterprise*, damaged by three bombs, work furiously to refuel, resupply and reposition her own aircraft and those from the stricken *Hornet*. Note the gun crew, closed-up in the foreground.

At 09:00 hours the *Enterprise* was screened by a providential rain squall, so that the *Hornet* attracted the attack. First hit on the flight deck aft, she was then shaken by two near misses. A crippled aircraft clipped her funnel, crashed and penetrated her flight deck, then exploded. Two torpedoes from low-flying "Kates" hit her amidships. As the ship came to a halt, she took three further bombs and was crashed by another aircraft.

In return, the American dive-bombers caught up with the *Shokaku* in company with the already damaged *Zuiho*. Five 227kg/500lb bombs now put the larger carrier out of the action. Both, however, survived.

Nagumo's second blow, of 44 aircraft, concentrated on the yet undamaged *Enterprise*. Despite a doughty defence she took three bombs but succeeded in evading nine torpedoes.

Beyond Nagumo lurked a fourth Japanese carrier, the *Junyo*. Her own 29-plane strike hit the *Enterprise* group at 11:20 hours but succeeded only in damaging the escort. Unable to return to their carrier, *Hornet*'s aircraft landed either on the *Enterprise*, or flew to nearby Espiritu Santo.

Throughout the afternoon, crews battled to save the stricken *Hornet*, now under tow. Repeat small-scale formations from the *Zuikaku* and the *Junyo* hit her piecemeal with a further torpedo and two bombs. With the enemy fleet uncomfortably close, she

could not be saved and was abandoned. Defying all efforts by her escort to sink her, her hulk had to be abandoned to the enemy, who sank her with torpedoes.

Although the Japanese lost other tonnage, all their carriers survived the Santa Cruz action. They had failed in their objective of seizing Guadalcanal, now of symbolic importance to both sides, but had claimed the valuable scalp of the *Hornet*. She had died hard, but her loss left the Americans desperately short of carriers.

Battle of the Philippine Sea

The year 1943 had transformed the situation in the Pacific, with a sequence of island-hopping Allied amphibious operations that gathered even more momentum in the following year. In June 1944, it was the turn of the Marianas, with the island of Saipan the objective.

By this time, too, the US Navy had established a powerful preponderance of aircraft carriers, nine *Essex*-class carriers (CVs) having been completed in parallel with nine *Independence*-class light carriers (CVLs).

Covering the amphibious fleet off Saipan was Admiral Raymond A. Spruance's Fifth Fleet, which included seven battleships, seven CVs and eight CVLs, deploying nearly 900 aircraft in total. With orders to destroy this armada "with one blow" was Vice-Admiral Ozawa Jisaburo's Mobile Fleet, whose five battleships were complemented by five fleet and four light carriers, with some 430 aircraft.

On June 18, Ozawa's fleet was crossing the Philippine Sea to attack Spruance from the west. Having aircraft of longer endurance, his plan was to stay beyond American range and to loose a series of air strikes that would hit the Fifth Fleet and fly on to Marianas airfields, there to refuel and rearm before raiding the Americans a second time in returning to their carriers.

Spruance's deputy, Vice Admiral Marc A. Mitscher had tactical control of the defence, his Fast Carrier Task Force (FT58) being divided into four task groups, typically of four carriers with a cruiser/destroyer escort.

Alerted to Ozawa's distant approach, Mitscher arranged his four groups in an "L" configuration with Vice Admiral Willis A. Lee's battleship task group TG.58.7 located in the angle.

TOP: **Riding at anchor at Majuro Atoll in the Marshalls, the Third/Fifth Fleet carriers are prominent. In the foreground is one of the distinctive *Independence*-class CVLs; in the distance is the veteran *Enterprise* and, beyond, *Essex*-class CVs.** ABOVE: **Desperately short of fuel, Fifth Fleet aviators are guided to their carriers by Admiral Mitscher famously burning their searchlights.**

All anti-aircraft guns were now supplied with proximity-fused ammunition and the carriers had, between them, 450 fighters. These were controlled by a fighter direction team experienced in meeting any combination of threat.

On June 19, between 10:00 and 15:00 hours, the Japanese hurled four waves of aircraft against this defence, which dissipated their efforts as a rock does a breaking sea. The first strike lost 42 aircraft from 69, the second 97 from 128. Those that went on to the island airfields found American intruder patrols overhead. The third wave became disorientated and, barely attacking, lost only 7 aircraft from 47, but the disastrous fourth lost 73 of 82. In the course of this massacre, Ozawa ran into an American submarine concentration, losing the carriers *Taiho* and *Shokaku*.

Having recovered about 100 aircraft Ozawa headed westward, followed by Spruance, less one carrier group. Finally sighting Ozawa at 15:40 hours on June 20, Mitscher launched 216 aircraft. These sank the carrier *Hiyo* and some tankers but, returning in darkness from maximum range, 80 aircraft ran out of fuel and ditched.

Ozawa had just 35 operational aircraft left but, mindful of his primary duty to protect the Saipan landings, Spruance did not press the pursuit to a conclusion, for which he attracted criticism.

Although the Japanese had lost three carriers, their greatest loss were the aircrew that manned the total of 426 aircraft destroyed. So overwhelming was Mitscher's success that his crews referred to it disparagingly as the "Marianas Turkey Shoot". In return, the Fifth Fleet suffered no losses in ships but 130 aircraft had been destroyed, together with a comparatively modest 76 aircrew.

The Americans were producing not only thousands of replacement aircraft but similar numbers of aircrew. The Japanese could nowhere near match this, and the situation was that their remaining carriers were effectively inoperable until more aircrew could be trained. This, the Americans had no intention of giving them time to do.

TOP: **The *Essex*-class *Bunker Hill* suffers a near miss from an enemy aircraft (upper left) that has apparently had its tail shot off. A year later the carrier would be so damaged as to be beyond economical repair.** ABOVE: **An F6F Hellcat of the later, *Essex*-class *Yorktown* is readied for launch. Note that the pilot receives instructions by hand signal and by chalk board.** BELOW LEFT: **Having survived every major carrier battle to date the *Zuikaku* once again puts her faith in a smart use of the helm to come through. In the foreground, assisting in providing flak cover, is the rarely photographed cruiser *Oyodo*.**

"Falling like plums."
Reference to Japanese aircraft in the action report of a picket destroyer at the Battle of the Philippine Sea, June 19, 1944

ABOVE: **A distant view shows the *Shokaku* damaged and under concentrated attack. She survived this only to be destroyed by submarine torpedo.**

Leyte Gulf

Just four months after the Battle of the Philippine Sea, the Americans landed on the island of Leyte in the Philippines themselves. The Japanese mustered their full available fleet in an all-out effort to dislodge them. As ever, their plan involved complex moves but in essence depended upon the invasion beaches being hit simultaneously by heavy surface warfare groups issuing from straits to the north and south.

Covering the American operation was the Third Fleet, which was the Fifth Fleet's title when under its alternative C-in-C, Admiral William F. Halsey. To prevent its intervention, Halsey was to be lured away by the irresistible bait of the remaining Japanese carriers which, in the near-absence of aircrew after the Philippine Sea debacle, were effectively useless. Vice Admiral Ozawa's mission, therefore, was to use his carrier group to trail its coat well to the north-east of the islands, attracting Halsey away to allow Vice Admirals Kurita and Nishimura to advance through the archipelago from the west.

Both the latter groups were detected early and, on October 24, 1944, subjected to prolonged air attack, Kurita by Mitscher's carriers, Nishimura by the lesser power of the Seventh Fleet, Vice Admiral Kinkaid's shore support force and land-based aircraft.

> **"It was like a puppy being smacked by a truck."**
> **Officer of destroyer USS *Johnston* sunk by 356mm/14in salvo at the Battle of Samar, October 25, 1944**

TOP: **The Battle of Samar. Taffy 3's escort carriers and their escort attempt concealment with funnel and chemical smoke as salvoes from Admiral Kurita's force fall among them. The carriers had been left uncovered once Admiral Halsey allowed himself to be enticed away by Ozawa's Northern Force.** ABOVE: **Alone on a wide sea; a pilot's view of his ship. A second aircraft, a Curtiss SB2C Helldiver, can be seen leaving the deck of this unnamed *Essex*-class ship.**

During the night of October 24–25, Nishimura's force was eliminated in a crushing gun and torpedo action in the Surigao Strait. However, the northern arm of the Japanese pincer advanced as planned.

The Japanese strategy had succeeded brilliantly, for Halsey, believing his pilots' reports that they had effectively destroyed Kurita's group, headed north after Ozawa, failing to leave behind even a precautionary covering force.

Ozawa could muster about a score of fighters, whereas Mitscher had about 500 aircraft of all types. Four carriers, *Zuikaku*, *Zuiho*, *Chiyoda* and *Chitose*, were easily destroyed during October 25, but annihilation of the whole group was prevented by urgent calls for Halsey's return.

LEFT: **Kamikazes continued their depredations following the main actions. On October 29, off Leyte, the CVL *Belleau Wood* suffered 92 fatalities and lost 12 aircraft in this spectacular incident.** BELOW: **Apparently armed with a 500kg/1,102lb bomb a kamikaze A6M "Zeke" readies for take-off in October 1944. As the aircraft made one-way trips, their range was effectively doubled.**

LEFT: **Admiral Halsey's legendary aggressive nature got the better of him at Leyte Gulf, only his national popularity saving him from censure. Admiral Fisher's dictum "Hit First, Hit Hard, Keep Hitting" has been paraphrased on this wartime poster.** BELOW: **Trailing defensive gun smoke, the *Zuikaku* and a *Terutsuki*-class destroyer are seen under attack at the Battle of Cape Engaño. Both the *Zuikaku* and the CVL *Chitose*, in the background, were sunk.**

VICTORY BEGINS AT HOME!

Far to his south, the still-potent surface group of Kurita was, in the absence of the Third Fleet, heading southward down the coast of Samar. Between it and the vulnerable amphibious fleet lay only the unsuspecting escort carrier force of Rear Admiral Thomas L. Sprague. Attached to the Seventh Fleet, Sprague's 16 escort carriers (CVEs) were tasked mainly with close air support for forces ashore, but on the morning of October 25 they found themselves under fire from a force that included three battleships and six heavy cruisers.

One CVE is a useful unit but of limited potential. However, 16 CVEs together are much more formidable, deploying about 250 F4F Hellcats and 190 TBF/TBM Avengers. Organized in three groups, the force overcame its initial shock to hurl every available aircraft, armed or unarmed, against the apparently overwhelming force of Kurita. Their attacks gradually became more coordinated and were supported valiantly by Sprague's destroyer escort.

The scale and fury of Sprague's defence convinced Kurita that he was, after all, facing Mitscher's Third Fleet carriers and, after indecisive and largely ineffective action, he withdrew.

During this, the Battle of Samar, the Americans lost two CVEs and three escorts, the Japanese three heavy cruisers. For the first time, the Americans were then subjected to organized kamikaze tactics by land-based enemy aircraft.

Halsey, having been recalled, arrived too late to intercept Kurita's retreat but the Leyte landings had been saved from interference by Sprague's action.

After Leyte Gulf, the Imperial Japanese Fleet ceased to be a factor that could influence the outcome of the Pacific War. It had been defeated, not in classic surface action but by the medium of carrier-based air power.

ABOVE: **Although a decade in development, the Douglas A3D Skywarrior did not enter service as a carrier-based, nuclear-capable bomber until 1956. Its size and weight was a convincing argument for larger carriers.** LEFT: **Considered cramped even by 1945 standards, the *Essex*-class carriers nonetheless continued to be valuable assets, and most were subjected to one or more modernizations. This is *Intrepid* (CV-11) in October 1968, having been fitted with a full angled deck.**

Post-war aircraft carrier developments

As World War II ended, the pressure to increase the size of carriers was as strong as ever. Bristling arrays of 40mm/1.57in and 20mm/0.79in anti-aircraft (AA) weapons had proved inadequate to stop the kamikaze which, often shredded and with the pilot dead, still had the momentum to follow a ballistic course to its target. The short-term solution was the adoption of the fast-firing 76.2mm/3in 70-calibre gun which could disintegrate the machine but this was only a stop-gap pending the introduction of the surface-to-air missile (SAM), with its associated bulky directors, launchers, storage and loading gear.

In 1945 the Cold War began and, during its earlier years, the prospects of nuclear war were very real. Before the introduction of the nuclear submarine (1952) and the nuclear-tipped Polaris intercontinental ballistic missile, or ICBM (1960), the most practical means of delivering a nuclear weapon into Soviet Russian heartland was the carrier-based bomber. Such aircraft were seriously large, the original being the 23,977kg/52,860lb North American AJ Savage, delivered from 1949. From 1956, this was superseded by the 37,195kg/82,000lb, jet-propelled Douglas A3D Skywarrior. Their spans, respectively, were 22.91m/75ft 2in and 22.1m/72ft 6in.

Even before the introduction of these monsters, with their increased demands on catapults and landing space, much thought was being devoted to the optimization of flight deck

ABOVE: ***Ark Royal* (III)'s new steam catapult being proofed by a Westland Wyvern from a shore-based trials unit. The extra power of steam catapults enabled smaller carriers to launch heavier aircraft.**

procedures, the importance of which had been demonstrated in the pre-1945 "deck-load" air strikes.

The revolutionary, but simple, answer was first proposed in August 1951. By angling the flight path from starboard quarter to port bow, aircraft would no longer be at risk in fouling the island. A large parking area was also created, starboard side forward, and any aircraft that jumped the arresters or crash barrier no longer ran on into the deck park. Indeed, the pilot could simply hit the throttle and go around again. This "angled deck" was also clear of the forward-mounted catapults, which could be used even while aircraft were landing-on.

First trials of the angled deck were conducted during 1951 by HMS *Triumph*, which had it simply painted on to her axial deck. Similar work with the *Midway* led the Americans in 1952 to make the first physical conversion, aboard the *Antietam*.

Existing hydro-pneumatic and cordite-powered catapults were also nearing their practical limits. The idea of using steam power had been proposed during the 1930s and this concept, allied to wartime German work on long, slotted cylinders, led to a prototype steam catapult being trialled aboard HMS *Perseus* in 1951. Again the US Navy quickly took up the idea, the USS *Hancock* being the first recipient of a steam catapult in 1954, this being capable of launching a 31,751kg/70,000lb aircraft at 200kph/124mph.

Introduced in 1954 was the third British innovation to be universally adopted. Faster approaches and the nose-up landing attitude of some aircraft made it difficult for pilots to see and act upon the signals of the Deck Landing Officer (DLO), or "Batman". The Mirror Landing Aid replaced the DLO with a stabilized assembly which reflected his own landing light back to a pilot in the approach path. Suitable mirror/lens arrangements made it possible to inform the pilot that his line was correct, not high or low, nor to one side.

The latter three innovations together revolutionized deck operations and in particular facilitated the emergence of the American "super carrier".

ABOVE: The *Essex*-class *Lexington* (CV-16) seen in a late conversion to an attack carrier. With a full angled deck she could operate A-3 Skywarriors, A-4 Skyhawks and F-8 Crusaders. Prominent here are the Rotodomes of two early-warning E-2 Hawkeyes.

LEFT: A welcome sight to returning aviators, the Deck Landing Officer (DLO), otherwise the "Batman", used a standard range of signals (with personal variation depending upon the heat of the moment) to guide an aircraft to safe touchdown. Note the windbreak/sightscreen, the "steadier" and the communications number. ABOVE: The Mirror Landing Aid replaced the DLO. From the reflection of his landing lights a pilot could verify his altitude and height, while the two lateral rows of lights indicated his axial alignment.

LEFT: **For peacetime operation and under conditions of limited warfare the British Light Fleet Carrier proved to be flexible and economical. The Royal Navy could never maintain more than one off Korea. The *Ocean*, here seen with a deck-load of Sea Furies and Fireflies, arrived for her first tour in May 1951.** BELOW: **The Hawker Sea Fury was the last piston-engined fighter to be operated by the Fleet Air Arm. It also served in Korea aboard the Australian carrier *Sydney* and the example shown here is in Australian colours.** BOTTOM: **The *Boxer* (CV-21) was one of several *Essex*-class carriers to serve in Korea. Seen here largely as she was in 1945, before the days of angled decks, it is apparent how vulnerable the massed forward deck park was to any overshoot on the part of a landing aircraft.**

Carriers in the Korean War

North Korea's invasion of the Republic of Korea (South Korea) on June 25, 1950, precipitated the first war to involve a coalition fighting under the United Nations (UN) flag. The war was primarily land-based and its course is not, therefore, relevant to this account. Korea, however, has an extensive coastline for its size, permitting warships to intervene effectively, particularly as the invaders possessed no reckonable navy.

Already in the theatre were the Japan-based US Seventh Fleet and the forces of the British C-in-C, Far East. Both services were now Cold War oriented and had run down their Far Eastern presence to token levels. Initially, the Americans

> Planeguard duty for British carriers off Korea was, for destroyers, a boring and repetitive chore. When so detailed, the Canadian destroyer *Athabaskan* signalled "St Luke, Chapter 22, Verse 42." This turned out to be "Father, if thou be willing, remove this cup from me; nevertheless, not my will, but thine be done."

there could muster little more than a carrier group, built around the solitary *Valley Forge* (CV-45). Even more thinly supported was the British "Light Fleet" carrier *Triumph*.

Greatly outnumbered, the forces ashore required close air support, with deeper incursions to hit strategic targets, particularly communications. Airfields for land-based aircraft were practically non-existent so that the US Air Force had to work from bases in Japan or Okinawa. Cross-service agreement made the Air Force responsible for strategic targeting, but post-war training had emphasized air combat, so that aircraft carriers assumed the tasking.

On July 3, 1950, the two carriers operated in concert for a first operation, although it was largely symbolic for the ships as aircraft and operating procedures differed markedly.

Post-war, the British Fleet Air Arm (FAA) had shifted back to mainly home-produced aircraft, the usual mix being Seafire fighters (later, Sea Fury) and Firefly strike aircraft. Larger and faster, the *Valley Forge* deployed the then standard American combination of Grumman F9F Panthers (the first navy jet-propelled fighters to see combat), F4U Corsairs and AD Skyraiders. Both latter types were piston-engined but robust and versatile.

Despite experiences of World War II, the FAA still manifested relative matériel shortcomings. The Light Fleet could more economically deploy much the same air group as an armoured fleet carrier but proved to be too slow, cramped, and prone to weather damage and mechanical breakdown following extended tours on duty. Their aircraft, especially the Seafire, lacked the robustness of the Americans and, being of shorter range, were more limited in choice of targets. In contrast, the F4U and AD would stagger into the air hung about with bombs, rockets and napalm, yet still give four or more hours of close support.

Both navies operated helicopters for the first time in war. The Americans used the Sikorsky S-51 and S-55, the British only the former, known by them as the Dragonfly. Despite their limited performance, these early machines provided a new level of versatility, not least in their releasing an escort from the restricting duty of planeguard (i.e. to rescue pilots following overside flight deck accidents).

During the 37-odd months of the Korean War the Royal Navy was able to maintain just one Light Fleet on station at a time (and was pleased to accept Australia's offer of HMAS Sydney for one stint) for periods of up to seven months. Activity on-station was all-weather and unremitting, and the Light Fleets functioned so well because the enemy threat at sea was light to non-existent.

The US Navy's contribution was greater, building up to three, or even four, Essex-class carriers or light carriers (CVLs) on overlapping deployments, supported by escort carriers (CVEs) as available.

ABOVE: Replenishment-at-sea (RAS) greatly extends the period that a warship can remain operational. Having simultaneously delivered to the carrier Antietam (CV-36) and the battleship Wisconsin (BB-64), the ammunition ship Rainier (AE-5) accelerates away.

Carriers for sale

With the close of hostilities in 1945, the major powers all too quickly repolarized into East and West. The Cold War took grip, resulting by 1949 in the armed camps of the maritime-oriented North Atlantic Treaty Organization (NATO) and the predominantly military Warsaw Pact.

Greatly expanded during World War II, the navies of Britain and the United States were reluctant to dispose of their many, recently constructed capital ships, particularly the invaluable carriers, of which there had been too few to deter war.

Britain, impoverished by two major wars in thirty years, was in the grip of austerity yet still had obligations toward her remaining empire and NATO. The Naval Staff could justify two dozen and more "Light Fleet" or Intermediate carriers yet had not the funds to keep more than three or four in the active field. The large armoured fleet carriers, with their small aircraft capacity and large, expensive crews were thus phased out comparatively quickly. Surplus *Colossus*-class Light Fleets found their way into the Reserve Fleet trots, it being the intention of the Admiralty to complete the improved Majestics in slow time, releasing *Colossus*-class units for sale to offset the cost. With the rapid development of jet-propelled naval aircraft, however, the limitations of the Light Fleets in a shooting war became apparent and, with successive demands for fiscal cutbacks, ships of both classes were sold off, no Majestic ever serving in the Royal Navy.

TOP: **The *Independence*-class carriers were, for the US Navy, a means of creating further flight decks with fleet speed. They were too limited for peacetime use, however, and all were discarded or transferred. The *Cabot* went to Spain as the *Dédalo*, seen here in later years with V/STOL fighters forward.** ABOVE: **With the British government failing to provide the maritime strength necessary to protect Far Eastern imperial interests during World War II, Australia strengthened her own fleet post-1945. Two British "Light Fleets" were acquired on a permanent basis, the *Melbourne* being seen here.**

In accordance with the original plan, the *Colossus* herself went to France in 1946 as the *Arromanches*. In 1948 Australia took the *Terrible* (renamed *Sydney*) and Canada the *Magnificent*. Naval aviation appeared to have taken root when Australia then acquired the *Majestic* (renamed *Melbourne*) in

ABOVE: **The Indian carrier** *Vikrant* **(ex-HMS** *Hercules***) enters Grand Harbour, Malta, her new ownership evident from a modified radar fit and the mix of British and French-sourced aircraft.** RIGHT: **Following a period on loan to the Australian Navy, the British** *Colossus*-**class** *Vengeance* **was sold to Brazil in 1956 as the** *Minas Gerais.* **Used primarily for ASW, she is shown carrying Grumman S-2G Trackers, Agusta-built SH-3A Sea Kings and two Aerospatiale UH-13 Ecureuils.**

1955 and Canada the *Powerful* (renamed *Bonaventure*) in 1957. Canada, however, abandoned carrier operation in 1970, and Australia in 1985. The French, having also acquired the light carriers (CVLs) *Lafayette* and *Bois Belleau* from the United States, went on to design and build their own carriers.

Having gained experience with Merchant Aircraft Carriers (MAC) and an escort carrier (CVE), the Dutch purchased the *Venerable* (renamed *Karel Doorman*) in 1948. However, she was sold-on to Argentina in 1969. Here she joined the ex-*Warrior*, which had gone south in 1958. Traditional rivalries had already seen Brazil acquire the *Vengeance* (renamed *Minas Gerais*) in 1960, although Chile never joined this "club".

A final Light Fleet transfer was that of the *Hercules* to India in 1961. Renamed *Vikrant*, she proved to be the foundation for a permanent air-arm as India developed into the regional naval power.

While smaller British carriers thus proved valuable to many other fleets worldwide, the equivalent American ships, the CVLs, were not, in general, sold out. Besides the aforementioned pair purchased by France only one more, the *Cabot*, went foreign, being acquired by Spain in 1967 and renamed *Dédalo.*

That so few fleets went on to develop permanent air arms demonstrates the high cost of conventional fixed-wing carrier operation, a situation hardly changed by the introduction of V/STOL and helicopters.

ABOVE: **Although the Korean War was fought in the jet age, the participating "Light Fleets" of the British and Australian navies were still limited to Fireflies and Sea Furies which, nevertheless, gave an excellent account of themselves. Here, a Firefly AS5 of 817 Squadron touches down on the** *Sydney.*

73

Suez

When, following years of nationalist agitation against foreign presence in Egypt, President Nasser nationalized the Suez Canal on July 26, 1956, it provoked strong Anglo-French reaction. A plan was concocted whereby Israel would attack Egypt, whereupon Britain and France would demand a ceasefire and a withdrawal of the warring forces to lines ten miles from either side of the canal. Anglo-French elements would then occupy key positions. Failing agreement on these points, Britain and France would intervene militarily.

During a long build-up period, Britain reinforced the Mediterranean Fleet and assembled her sadly run-down amphibious warfare vessels at Malta, the nearest "friendly" point with adequate facilities. The Royal Air Force was also reinforced on its Cypriot bases, although their distance from Egypt meant that fighter cover would be practicable only if carrier-based. To intimidate the Egyptians, there was little attempt at concealing concentrations and considerable international opposition to the plan resulted, notably in Britain and the United States.

The British assembled three jet-capable carriers (*Eagle*, *Albion* and *Bulwark*) with a mix of nearly 90 Sea Hawk ground attack fighters, Sea Venom all-weather strike fighters and

TOP: **Preliminary bombing of strategic targets, such as oil storage tanks in Port Said, sent a clear message to the Egyptians of the futility of prolonged resistance.** ABOVE: **Royal Marine Commandos wait on the flight deck of the *Theseus* as the ship's 11 Navy Whirlwinds operate a short shuttle service to shore.**

turbo-prop Wyvern strike aircraft. The French carriers *Arromanches* and *Lafayette* added about 59 F4U Corsairs and TBF/TBM Avengers. None of these aircraft could match the performance of the Soviet-supplied MiG-15s of the Egyptian air force.

To the British force were added the Light Fleet carriers *Ocean* and *Theseus*. As training ships they were not equipped to operate aircraft, and their task would be to implement the strategy of "vertical envelopment", as being experimented with by the US Marine Corps. This involved the use of helicopters to insert spearhead troops, in conjunction with parachute drops, ahead of a main amphibious assault. To transport and land men of 45 Commando, the *Ocean* embarked six Sycamores and six Whirlwinds of the joint army/navy experimental helicopter unit, and the *Theseus* eleven FAA Whirlwinds.

Israel duly attacked on the evening of October 29. Twenty-four hours later Nasser rejected the Anglo-French ultimatum and RAF bombing began, together with selective light naval bombardment. With Egyptian resistance continuing, the strike carriers hit airfields on November 1, wiping out all aircraft on the ground not already evacuated.

Stiffening resistance brought forward the amphibious landing and, in a change of plan, it was to be preceded by an Anglo-French parachute drop with the, as yet, untried helicopter landing down-graded to reserve. The carrier strikes continued, meanwhile, seeking out troop, supply, and vehicle concentrations. Their aircraft then switched to close support during and following the parachute assault of November 5. On the following morning, 40 and 42 Commando went ashore and, with some armoured assistance, moved into the outskirts of Port Said.

The beaches had too shallow a declivity to permit Tank Landing Ships (LSTs) to use them. Wharfage was essential, therefore, and the helicopter assault was thus directed at placing 45 Commando in a suitable position to secure the fishing harbour. Despite the total inadequacy of these early helicopters for the task in hand, over 400 men and 20 tons of equipment were put ashore in a continuous shuttle.

At midnight on the same day, international pressure enforced a ceasefire. The operation was wound down as United Nations forces assumed control, the canal remaining closed for the ensuing six months due to the necessity of salvaging the many Egyptian block-ships.

Militarily, the campaign was successful and the extemporized helicopter assault led directly to the conversion and building of "commando carriers".

ABOVE LEFT: **Seen from an inbound LST (Landing Ship, Tank) assault landing craft and the *Ocean*'s six Whirlwind helicopters ferry troops ashore at Port Said.**

ABOVE: **Alongside in Port Said the *Ocean*, with a French hospital ship beyond, is seen with the Whirlwind helicopters that successfully proved the principle of "vertical envelopment" in an opposed situation.**

RIGHT: **As three Whirlwinds head shorewards from the *Ocean*, a second wave awaits the signal to lift off. A Royal Marine officer can be seen sitting in the door, with his map case and cradling his submachine-gun.**

ABOVE: **Sea Hawk fighters provided very effective close support to ground forces during the Suez operation. Two 227kg/500lb bombs could be carried on underwing hardpoints and armourers are here seen "bombing up" on one of the British carriers.**

The impact of helicopters

The advantages of aircraft supported by rotors rather than wings were apparent very early, the US Navy's first recorded interest being in 1916. At this stage, however, the concept was well ahead of practical reality and it would be the late 1930s before innovators such as Cierva, Focke-Achgelis and Sikorsky produced practical prototypes.

On May 13, 1940, the latter flew his VS-300 in free flight in a United States not yet involved in the European war. Circumstances, however, soon encouraged the helicopter's rapid development. By 1943, Sikorsky's VS-316 had become the world's first production model and, as the R-4, recorded a first under-weigh landing aboard the carrier Bunker Hill on May 7, 1943.

Still lacking power, early helicopters had little useful payload margin and, like early aircraft, were limited largely to observation. Extensive trials were conducted in flying from the deck of freighters to spot surfaced U-boats in the vicinity of convoys. Focke-Achgelis built wind-powered, man-carrying observation helicopters that could be assembled and towed behind surfaced U-boats.

Immediately post-war it was the R-4, as the Hoverfly I, which gave the British Fleet Air Arm (FAA) its first experience of rotor aircraft. Able both to hover and to cover large areas rapidly, there was obviously potential as an offensive anti-submarine warfare (ASW) platform. It needed little in the way

TOP: **A string of Bulwark's Westland Wessexes positions itself about its "spots" while a Type 82 frigate stands planeguard. Ships and helicopters have greatly influenced each other's design.** ABOVE: **Intended primarily for observation duties, the US Navy's Sikorsky HO3S-1 gave yeoman service during the Korean War and peacetime in the rapid rescue of ditched aviators, as of this F6F Hellcat.**

of flight deck, as demonstrated in 1946 by a successful landing on a destroyer. With the emerging Cold War emphasizing ASW, a whole new line of development was instigated.

An early success was the Bell HTL/HUL of 1946, widely used as a utility aircraft, for casualty evacuation and for transfers between ships. In the following year, the British firm of Westland began to build Sikorsky designs under licence, its Dragonfly corresponding to the American S-51, which saw considerable service in the Korean War. By now more reliable for use over water, helicopters appeared on aircraft carriers, their utility functions doubling with planeguard duty, thus releasing an escort ship for more appropriate employment.

Although the Sikorsky S-55 and S-58 (Westland's Whirlwind and Wessex) demonstrated considerable advances in capability during the 1950s and 1960s, they were too large to be considered for general ASW aboard flotilla ships.

For a frigate, the helicopter promised rapid, stand-off response to a submarine contact, but early machines such as the Westland Wasp were too small to carry the combined weight of sensors, weapons and data systems. The Americans sought to circumvent the problem by removing the crew, but the resulting Drone Anti-Submarine Helicopter (DASH) system was ahead of then-current technology, and proved unreliable.

The solution could lie only in either larger machines or in the operation of multiple smaller ones working as a team. This resulted in divergent development paths, with frigates being designed around ever-larger helicopters, ideally paired, and other aviation-capable ships such as the ASW helicopter carriers, commando carriers and amphibious warfare ships deploying them in numbers. The latter categories are also well able to fly ground attack helicopters such as the Apache, to compensate for their lack of the dedicated strike aircraft found aboard a conventional carrier. With their growing ability to operate V/STOL, and other novel forms of aircraft, such as the tilt-rotor V-22 Osprey, such ships are now blurring the once clear definition of what constitutes an "aircraft carrier".

TOP LEFT: **Carried for planeguard and utility duties, the Piasecki Vertol HUP-2 was also adapted for anti-submarine warfare. This picture, of Korean War vintage, shows an Essex class in near-original configuration and a McDonnell F2H Banshee.** ABOVE LEFT: **US naval interest in helicopters began late in 1943 with the acquisition (from the Army!) of 25 Sikorsky R-4Bs. Known in naval service as HNS-1s, they were used for pilot training.** ABOVE: **The latest British Iron Duke class of frigate is designed to carry a single anti-submarine Merlin in contrast to previous classes that had the advantage of carrying two of the smaller but less capable Westland Lynxes. The impact of the Merlin's size can be seen in the design of this frigate.** BELOW: **Carried typically aboard *Leander*-class frigates such as the *Aurora*, the Westland Wasp HAS.1 comprised the ship's major anti-submarine system. Note the two torpedoes carried by this machine, of 829 Squadron.**

Carrier jet aircraft developments

Although the first official all-jet landings were made soon after World War II (December 3, 1945, by a Sea Vampire on HMS *Ocean*, and July 21, 1946, by a McDonnell FH-1 Phantom I on USS *Franklin D. Roosevelt*) propeller-driven strike aircraft, at the peak of their development, remained in front-line service until after the Korean War (1950–53).

The first standard American jet carrier fighters were the McDonnell F2H Banshee and the F3H Demon. These would also have served alongside the big strategic bombers with augmented turboprop propulsion aboard the cancelled *United States* attack carrier (CVA-58).

The nuclear-capable attack bomber which actually entered service was the all-jet Douglas A3D (later A-3 Skywarrior), a 37,195kg/82,000lb aircraft which was introduced in 1957 and ended its time in reconnaissance and tanker roles. It operated from *Essex*- and *Midway*-class carriers as well as the giant Forrestal. Its supporting F3H Demons were superseded from 1962 by the outstanding F4H Phantom II, which acted both as fighter and as tactical strike aircraft.

The F4H (later F-4) served in tandem with the F8U (later F-8) Crusader, complementing an attack wing of "heavy" A-3s and "light" McDonnell Douglas A-4 Skyhawks. Already, the heavy investment required for developing new aircraft was forcing joint company projects, but the A-4 was particularly

TOP: **Dating from the early 1960s, the McDonnell Douglas F-4 Phantom was one of the best-ever carrier aircraft, being purchased also for the Royal Navy. This example has just been catapulted from the waist position aboard the American carrier *Independence* (CVA-62).** ABOVE: **In July 1950 the Grumman F9F Panther became the first Navy jet aircraft to see combat. Two Panthers are seen here on the catapults of the *Leyte* (CV-32). This *Essex*-class vessel is still in her original configuration: note the 127mm/5in gunhouses to the right.**

durable. By the late 1960s the offensive element was widened with a new medium attack aircraft, the Grumman A-6 Intruder, a 1,043kph/648mph twin-seat bomber that came also in tanker and electronic warfare variants.

From 1973 the F-4 was gradually superseded by another superlative Grumman fighter, the twin-seat F-14 Tomcat, the first to feature variable wing geometry. Ten years later it was complemented by the small and lighter McDonnell Douglas F/A-18 Hornet, a multi-purpose machine.

During the Korean War, the smaller British carriers operated only piston-engined aircraft alongside their jet-equipped American allies. Nonetheless, there were by 1953 four Fleet Air Arm (FAA) squadrons flying the 950kph/590mph Supermarine Attacker, an interim jet fighter based on the RAF's Spiteful. It was quickly superseded by the successful but slower Hawker Sea Hawk, a single-seat ground attack fighter.

By the late 1950s, the Supermarine Scimitar had been introduced. Although multi-role and nuclear-capable, it represented a major improvement in performance and range, but at the cost of twice the weight. It flew alongside a new Blackburn design, the Buccaneer, a low-level nuclear-capable strike aircraft of exceptionally strong construction. It served until the Royal Navy's carrier force was controversially eliminated with the retirement of the *Ark Royal* (III) in 1978. For her final decade in service the *Ark Royal* had to operate American-sourced F-4 Phantoms, due to the cancellation of a new British fighter.

Where, owing to the limited numbers involved, the British government no longer considers domestically developed carrier aircraft a viable proposition and has purchased the American Joint Strike Fighter for its projected new carriers, the French have no such inhibitions. For their new carriers of the early 1960s they produced the durable Dassault Etendard fighter-bombers. More recently, for their confident new *Charles de Gaulle* carrier they have introduced the Dassault Rafale fighter, although production has been much delayed.

With the end of the Cold War, carrier-on-carrier actions have become only remote possibilities. The accent is now upon intervention and it may be assumed that future carrier aircraft will continue the priorities of air superiority and ground support, but with an increasing emphasis on stealth.

TOP: **On December 3, 1945 a converted deHavilland Vampire I made the first-ever landing by a pure jet aircraft aboard a carrier. Further strengthened, the aircraft went into limited production as the F.20 Sea Vampire. The carrier was the** *Ocean*, **a British "Light Fleet".** ABOVE: **Another Grumman success story was the F-14 Tomcat, the US Navy's first variable-geometry fighter. Designed to establish "air superiority", this example is carrying six Phoenix air-to-air missiles, long-range weapons capable of reaching beyond 180km/110 miles.**

ABOVE: **In various configurations, the Grumman A-6 Intruder has served in the US Navy long and well. Its primary role was as an attack bomber, in which service it could carry a 7,855kg/17,280lb bomb load.** LEFT: **Touchdown. The elegant McDonnell Douglas F/A-18 Hornet is a multi-role fighter flown by both Navy and Marine pilots. Capable of Mach 1.8 speed, it entered squadron service in 1983.**

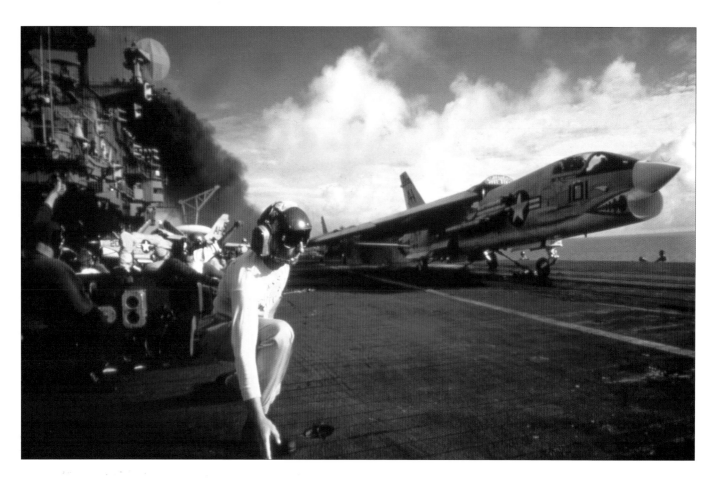

Naval air power in Vietnam

During the early 1960s, Communist insurgents from North Vietnam were freely infiltrating neighbouring South Vietnam via the contiguous border with Laos. To buttress the South's democratic government, and to register overt disapproval, the United States maintained a naval presence offshore. Its frequent reconnaissance overflights and inshore incursions in pursuit of signal intelligence finally provoked North Vietnamese light forces to tangle with American destroyers in August 1964. A retaliatory two-carrier air strike opened what was to prove a ten-year, unwinnable conflict.

With widespread public approval, Congress authorized President Johnson "to take all necessary measures … to prevent further aggression". Rapid reinforcement of two further carriers resulted in the immediate transfer of Chinese MiG jet fighters to bases around the North's capital, Hanoi.

As North Vietnamese activities continued unabated, the president, in December 1964, authorized a structured action plan. Air strikes against the Laotian infiltration routes would first warn Hanoi. If the hint were to be ignored, these would be extended to lines of communication inside North Vietnamese

TOP: **An LTV F-8 Crusader fighter awaits catapulting from the *Constellation* (CVA-64). Squadron deliveries for the aircraft were between 1957 and the late 1960s, with many earlier machines being successively modernized.**

ABOVE: **One result of the carrier operations off Vietnam was the life extension of the Douglas AD-1 Skyraider. By 1957 this highly versatile design was 12 years old. Universally known as the Spad, it is seen here in the A-1H single-seat low-level bombing version.**

> "Two SAMs, two o'clock low. Break right! Break right!"
> One naval pilot warning another during a low-level
> incursion over North Vietnam

borders. A final escalation, if proved necessary, would target the North's airfields and fuel resources, while ports would be mined and blockaded. From the outset, however, for fear of Chinese or Soviet intervention, rules of engagement were suffocatingly constricting.

TOP: **As in Korea, air power in Vietnam was vested in the aircraft carrier. Here, the *Enterprise* (CVAN-65) is seen launching an air strike. The world's first nuclear-powered carrier, she is still in her original configuration.** LEFT: **While it seemed improbable that the AD could ever be replaced by a jet-powered aircraft with similar versatility, McDonnell Douglas succeeded with the A-4 Skyhawk. It entered service in 1956 and, many variants later, was still giving a good account of itself in the 1982 Falklands War.** ABOVE: **The extensive mining of Haiphong and essential Vietnam waterways entailed, following cessation of hostilities, the massive Operation Endsweep. Aboard the *Inchon* (LPH-12) can be seen RH-53As, CH-53A Sea Stallions, re-equipped for mine clearing, June 1973.**

This was to be an aerial offensive, to be shared between the Seventh Air Force and carriers of Task Force 77 (TF77). To avoid overlap, North Vietnam and Laos were divided into target areas, or "route packages". Those "Up North" would be hit by carriers based on the so-called "Yankee Station", just south of Hainan Island, while those in Laos would receive attention from "Dixie Station" off the South Vietnamese coast.

The opening phases, "Barrel Roll" and "Steel Tiger", comprised armed reconnaissance missions over Laos. Their main result was that surface-to-air missile (SAM) sites began to appear. Because Soviet and Chinese technicians were likely to be involved, attacks during the vulnerable installation phase were banned.

SAMs, particularly the SA-2, became a major threat. They enforced high-speed, low-level flying, beneath radar coverage but within range of barrage fire from automatic weapons. This was far more deadly than enemy MiGs.

Yet having no effect, the American policy was extended to phase two in February 1965. This, code-named "Rolling Thunder", was a sustained bombing campaign of selected strategic targets, avoiding Hanoi and the principal port of Haiphong. For the first time, guided bombs were deployed against precision targets and cluster bombs on soft-skinned targets such as transport concentrations or dumps. On several occasions, the campaign was stood down to give the enemy an opportunity to negotiate. Each time, with no response, it was resumed with the "bomb line" extending ever nearer to the Chinese border and to ever more sensitive targets.

With the proliferation of SAM and associated flak sites, "Iron Hand", highly hazardous suppression strikes, had to be undertaken frequently.

In March 1972, the North Vietnamese army invaded the South in strength and now-President Nixon ordered Haiphong and strategic waterways to be mined. Over 11,000 were laid.

The ceasefire of January 1973 brought a generally unsatisfactory campaign to a close. TF77 carriers' contribution had been enormous, with 21 separate ships making a total of 86 deployments. A total of 859 aircraft were lost from all causes and some 620 aircrew were listed dead, missing or captured. Many more were saved by the crews of the Helicopter Combat Support Squadrons. In terms of operational experience, the campaign was invaluable.

Carrier battle groups and tactics

Even by the onset of World War II, it was realized, particularly by the Japanese and American navies, that the aircraft carrier was no longer just the handmaiden of the battle line but an offensive unit in her own right. Her independence was emphasized by her requirement even when equipped with catapults, to "chase the wind" to launch and recover her aircraft. Needing thus to leave the mutual security of the main group, she also needed her own dedicated escort.

As we have seen, the naval war in the Pacific became, increasingly, one of carriers seeking mutual destruction. Their mighty blows, each hoping to be the first to land, were aimed at each other, leaving the gun-armed fleet as bystander if not actively involved in the carrier's defence.

The carrier battle group became the choice tactical formation but, in the early days, when just two to four carriers were available, an admiral had to choose whether to concentrate them for maximum offensive effort or to disperse them for improved concealment and survivability. This could depend simply on the available number of escorts. The Japanese might place a small carrier group ahead in order to divert the initial strike from the major group following some distance behind.

A full deck-load strike was reckoned to stand a good chance of disabling an enemy through damaging her flight deck if not actually sinking her. This is reflected in the composition of air wings for, as the disparity in carrier strength grew ever more decisively in the American's favour, their proportion of fighters grew from 25 to 65 per cent.

With fifteen or more carriers at his disposal, Mitscher grouped them in threes and fours with common escort. Three

TOP: **With no fixed-wing, conventional carriers remaining, the Royal Navy was reduced by the early 1980s to forming task groups around a V/STOL carrier. The *Invincible* is seen here in 1983, supported by a Type 12 frigate, two Leanders, a tanker and two multi-purpose store ships.** ABOVE: **Altogether a more formidable proposition, US Navy carrier battle groups, here centred on the *Kitty Hawk* (CVA-63), have the benefit of three-dimensional radar, airborne early warning and aircraft the equal of anything ashore. Trailing the group, unadvertised, will be a supporting nuclear submarine.**

of four Task Groups thus comprised a Task Force which was, effectively, the whole fleet less the fast battleships, to be used as a sort of mobile reserve.

At the time of the Battle of the Philippine Sea the sheer number of carriers, although deploying two-thirds fighters, could still muster an adequate offensive power while maintaining a defensive cover that simply overwhelmed the attackers.

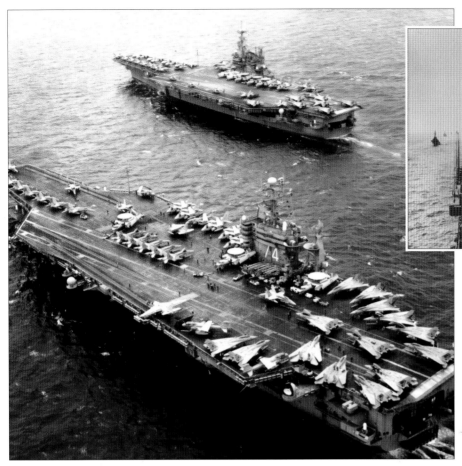

ABOVE: **Despite post-World War II fleet rundown, Task Force 77, the US Navy's main presence off the Korean peninsula, was boosted with the arrival of new carriers. The *Philippine Sea* (CV-47) and another Essex class are visible over the deck park of the *Boxer* (CV-21).** LEFT: **Hard to believe, but 37 years separate the commissioning dates of the conventionally powered *Independence* (CV-62/ 1959) and the nuclear-powered *John C. Stennis* (CVN-74/1996). In terms of dimensions and aircraft capability, they differ little.** BELOW LEFT: **A lone Liberty ship stands silhouetted against the result of one of the post-war Bikini tests. The weight alone of the water in the column was sufficient to crush and swamp a conventional ship, and the possible use of tactical nuclear weapons required task groups to be more dispersed.** BELOW: **The atomic explosion to the left could easily encompass this 1955 task group. Here, the *Platte* (AO24) simultaneously refuels the *Essex*-class *Philippine Sea* (CV-47) and a *Fletcher*-class destroyer, the Watts DD-567.**

Radar now detected an incoming strike early enough for the escort, now often including a battleship, to close in a defensive ring. If the attackers escaped the Combat Air Patrol (CAP) at a distance, they then ran into a close-in barrage of proximity-fused ammunition.

The resulting attrition in Japanese aircrew led directly to the kamikaze. With a pilot no longer concerned for his survival, probability swung again in favour of the attacker. This strengthened arguments in favour of the larger carrier, supporting improved horizontal protection and a "beefed-up" armament, with greater inherent survivability.

By 1945, the big tactical groups of carriers and amphibious warfare craft dominated the Pacific war. A rethink was, however, in order with the advent of the Cold War and the very real possibility of nuclear weapon deployment. Even without particularly accurate delivery, its blast could sink or disable an entire group. Greater dispersion, although a solution, only increased the vulnerability to more likely conventional attack. This conundrum has a solution which must depend upon the nature of the threat at any specific time.

With the gradual diminishing of the number of available carriers, each becomes more significant. Her offensive capacity is eroded if her mission requires her also to deploy a credible anti-submarine component, in addition to airborne early warning, tankers, electronic warfare and utility aircraft. Accommodating all this, however, forces up the size of the carrier and, fortuitously, the larger the dimensions the greater the ability to absorb punishment while remaining operational.

The introduction of V/STOL

For a proven concept with obvious application, Vertical or Short Take-Off and Land (V/STOL) had a slow and difficult transition to naval use. It began with the Cold War assumption that the West's airfields and fixed aerial assets would be targeted and made unusable. Although some small supersonic aircraft could then still operate from suitable lengths of highway a V/STOL aircraft, using vectored thrust, could in theory require an area no larger than a tennis court. On this basis, the British Hawker company produced the prototype P.1127 (later "Kestrel") in 1960 and this, refined to the GR.1 version of the Harrier, entered RAF squadron service in October 1969.

In February 1966 an economy-driven Defence Review precipitated a run-down of British military presence "East of Suez", with the specious corollary that there would be no future role for aircraft carriers. The attack carrier CVA-01 was cancelled and no existing carrier would be replaced on its retirement. From the "mid-1970s" the Fleet Air Arm (FAA) would become all-helicopter.

Three years before, however, the prototype Kestrel had been demonstrated aboard the *Ark Royal* and, perhaps more significantly, had landed in 1966 aboard the commando carrier *Bulwark*, which could no longer handle conventional fixed-wing aircraft, deploying only helicopters.

Studies began for a ship combining the required facility for command and control with an area-defence SAM system and flight deck and accommodation for Sea King anti-submarine warfare (ASW) helicopters. The navy quietly extended the studies to complement the helicopters with V/STOL. Because the government could no longer consider a "carrier", the ship became a "command carrier", or "through-deck cruiser". Surprisingly, the project survived to the stage of the ordering, in 1973, of the ship that would become the *Invincible*.

It was fortunate that, in 1969, the less cash-strapped US Marine Corps had placed a substantial order for modified Harriers, maintaining the aircraft's high profile, but it was to be 1975 before studies were funded into what would become the Sea Harrier. The prototype made a first landing aboard the *Hermes* in November 1978 and entered FAA squadron service in good time to join the *Invincible*, completed in July 1980.

BOTTOM: **In February 1963 the new Hawker P.1127, provisionally named the Kestrel, landed aboard the *Ark Royal* (III) and, four months later, operated from the commando carrier *Bulwark*. The long-term future of the Royal Navy's conventional carriers was already doubtful and the slow metamorphosis of the Kestrel to the Sea Harrier was one of great significance.** BELOW: **By its adoption of the aircraft, the United States Marine Corps rescued the Harrier from politically induced oblivion. This example gets airborne from the flight deck of the amphibious assault ship *Nassau* (LHA-4).**

Britain's last fixed-wing carrier, *Ark Royal*, had paid off in 1978 but the *Invincible*, carrier-manqué, together with the *Hermes*, proved the continuing validity of fighter cover for the fleet during the Falklands War of 1982. Here, they operated RAF ground-attack Harriers alongside FAA fighter variants.

V/STOL (or, better, STOVL, for that is the preferred mode of operation) is no substitute for the high-performance, purpose-designed fighter. Its engine, designed to deliver sufficient vectored thrust to support the aircraft's weight, is over-large and uneconomical for long-duration cruising as, necessarily, is the aircraft's configuration.

Limited-performance fighters are, however, infinitely superior to no fighters at all, and the concept is therefore appealing to fleets that cannot afford the cost of developing and sustaining large conventional carriers. Importantly, as far as evolution is concerned, V/STOL has enabled a whole range of hybrid vessels, particularly in amphibious warfare, to deploy significant air defence and ground attack capability.

During the Falklands emergency of 1982 large roll-on, roll-off ships and container ships were also proven to be capable of carrying and, if necessary, deploying Harriers. The associated Arapaho project embraced the "containerization" of all related support services and the provision of sectioned, prefabricated take-off pads. Between them, V/STOL and rotor flight have effectively blurred the definition of what constitutes an "aircraft carrier", enabling specialist large assault ships to provide organic close air support for their operations.

ABOVE: **The need to justify the *Invincible* as a "through-deck cruiser" left her flight deck area significantly reduced by the Sea Dart area defence surface-to-air missile launcher and its guidance radars.** LEFT: **With the dissolution of the old Soviet Union, its armed forces suffered sudden reduction and a starvation of funding. The navy and its rapidly evolving conventional carrier capability were not spared and the future of such technologically advanced aircraft as the Yak-141 is far from certain.** BELOW LEFT: **The United Kingdom government is no longer willing to support an aviation industry capable of producing novel military aircraft. New aircraft are thus either the result of participation in international partnerships or are, like the F-35 Joint Strike Fighter, purchased directly.** BELOW: **The *Tarawa*-class amphibious assault ships are multi-purpose and, weighing-in at nearly 40,642 tonnes/40,000 tons full load, have a spacious flight deck capable easily of undertaking V/STOL operation. Here, a Marine Corps AV-8B leaves the *Belleau Wood* (LHA-3).**

Argument – large or small carriers?

Naval aviation, in the shape of Conventional Take-Off and Land (CTOL) carriers, is staggeringly expensive, yet it is abundantly clear that any fleet with pretensions to "blue water" capability cannot function without it. Once the decision is made to acquire carriers, however, battle is joined and argument rages – what represents the best value for money, one or two large vessels or several smaller? Here, the American experience is enlightening, for the US Navy has been building large carriers in an unbroken line of development for a half century. With almost each new acquisition, another but similar argument erupts and, again, the big ship has to be justified.

In studies, four sizes of carrier were considered: (1) a 91,444-tonne/90,000-ton or more carrier or nuclear carrier (CV/CVN); (2) a 40,642–60,963-tonne/40,000–60,000-ton carrier, vertical take-off and land (CVV), capable of operating conventional and vertical or short take-off and land (V/STOL) aircraft; (3) a 20,321–35,562-tonne/20,000–35,000-ton VSS capable of operating V/STOL in all modes; and (4) a less than 20,321-tonne/20,000-ton ship unclassified, capable of operating V/STOL only in the vertical mode.

Category (1) ships can include about nine types of aircraft in their inventory, and a reduction in size to category (2) would mean the loss of heavy long-range interceptors of the size of the F-14 Tomcat.

All else being equal, a 335m/1,099ft, 91,444-tonne/90,000-ton ship compared with a 275m/902ft, 50,802-tonne/50,000-ton

TOP: **Large carriers are more cost effective and more survivable, but are staggeringly expensive to acquire and maintain.** ABOVE: **Short take-off, vertical land (STOVL) is allied to small waterplane area, twin hull (SWATH) in this concept small carrier, designed to give a steady platform in poor weather.**

vessel will have only 22 per cent greater dimensions yet 82 per cent more volume. Volume is the most critical parameter when designing to accommodate aircraft, magazine/fuel stowage and propulsion machinery.

Larger hulls are more easily driven. At 30 knots, a 91,444-tonne/90,000-ton vessel requires only one-third the horsepower per ton of a destroyer. A larger ship can continue to operate her aircraft in a higher sea state than a smaller one, while her overall accident rate is about half.

ABOVE: **This Thornycroft concept for a STOVL carrier dates from 1976, before ski-jumps were introduced. In comparison with a large carrier, her cost per ton would be significantly greater.** LEFT: **Concept drawings of STOVL fighter and airborne early warning AEW aircraft. The extra machinery weight, its complexity and its effects on aerodynamics will always mean that a STOVL aircraft will be an inferior performer compared with a conventional one.** BELOW: **An American concept for a small STOVL carrier. Note the landing spots aft and the angled take-off path which gives parking space forward of and abaft the island.** BOTTOM: **Resurrecting the old airship "skyhook" concept, this idea for a Harrier carrier entails the aircraft using excessive fuel in the hover mode. It also seems to be an awful lot of ship for very little aviation.**

In establishing sea superiority, the VSS compares badly with the CVV, its air wing being 30 against 50. Able to ship an anti-submarine warfare (ASW) component, the CVV could operate singly in all but a high-threat environment. In contrast, the VSS could operate singly in only low-threat situations and would require an ASW escort.

A 40,642-tonne/40,000-ton VSS could deploy about 30 aircraft, but a 20,321-tonne/20,000-ton ship only 8. Her capacity for self defence is low and she would require a capable, missile-armed escort. Ships of the smallest size would be able to operate V/STOL only in the uneconomical vertical take-off and land (VTOL) mode, reducing mission capability by nearly 50 per cent. The demands of a flight of, say, four aircraft would effectively squeeze out other roles for the ship.

Nuclear propulsion puts about 30 per cent more on the initial price of a ship but internal space thus saved enables her to stow four times as much aviation fuel and three times the ordnance. A nuclear ship can steam at high speed almost indefinitely and, while being free of tanker support herself, can offer limited fuel oil for her escorts. She has no smoke problem. Extra support costs appear to be of the order of three per cent.

In the face of enemy action, the larger carrier is the less vulnerable. Her extra size and compartmentalization enable her better to absorb penetration and shock. Her torpedo protection is more comprehensive and, if damaged, she has greater stability margins and more watertight subdivision. Not least, her extra aircraft make it less likely that she will be damaged in the first place. Initial cost per ton will be less but both air wing and through-life expenditure are considerable.

Assault carriers

For amphibious warfare, the introduction of atomic weapons made speed of operation paramount, to clear the beach and to disperse shipping. The US Marine Corps (USMC) saw in the helicopter the means of, eventually, putting ashore a complete division but, in the early 1950s, the vision was ahead of the technology. Nonetheless, by 1956, Sikorsky had produced the HR25 helicopter, capable of lifting 20 equipped troops.

For the envisaged division, considerable sea transport would be required and the USMC requested the conversion of suitable reserve escort carriers (CVEs). Only one, however, was forthcoming, the *Thetis Bay* (CVE-90) emerging as the helicopter assault carrier CVHA-1 in July 1956 following limited modification for what was a temporary role.

In Britain these developments had been followed with interest and, in November 1956, the first such "vertical envelopment" operation was undertaken during the Suez intervention. Here, using an ad hoc collection of totally inadequate helicopters, two unconverted Light Fleet carriers took just 82 minutes to put ashore over 400 men and 23.4 tonnes/23 tons of stores at a selected point. This resulted in the conversion of the *Bulwark* and *Albion* to "commando carriers" in 1960 and 1962 respectively. In this role they could accommodate 750–900 troops and 16 helicopters.

The *Thetis Bay* could carry 22 helicopters but "spot" only five at a time. Exercises showed the unsuitability of CVEs for more elaborate conversion. Three *Essex*-class carriers (CVs)

TOP: **Helicopters and V/STOL are complemented in the large assault ship, the one to give assault mobility, the other to provide limited ground support and fighter cover. This example is the *Nassau* (LHA-4).** ABOVE: **Even as the *Albion* and *Bulwark* proved the "commando carrier" concept for the Royal Navy, so did the *Essex*-class *Boxer* (CV-21) for the US Navy. Beyond landing most of her light anti-aircraft weapons, she appears little modified.**

thus acted as interim assault carriers until a designed-to-task ship could be produced. This was the Amphibious Assault Helicopter Carrier (LPH) of which the *Iwo Jima* and six sisters were completed between August 1961 and June 1970. At 17,273 tonnes/17,000 tons they were smaller than the British pair yet could support a full marine battalion of 2,100 men together with 32 assorted helicopters. The Bulwarks did, however, carry four vehicle and personnel landing craft (LCVPs) under davits, allowing heavy material to be put ashore. Lacking these, the Iwo Jimas were limited to the 2,858kg/6,300lb that could be slung beneath a CH-46 helicopter.

The last of the class was fitted for a pair of LCVPs but the ships' general limitations for assault operations in poor weather resulted in a rethink. What emerged in 1976 to 1980 was the

ABOVE LEFT: **An unusual view of the after end of the *Nassau* (LHA-4's) flight deck, seen from flight control. It will be apparent that the superstructure, unlike the island of a conventional carrier, extends almost to the centreline.** ABOVE: **Sikorsky HUS-1/UH-34D Seahorses of US Marine Corps Squadron HMM-262 take off from an *Iwo Jima*-class LPH in the early 1960s during a training exercise.** LEFT: ***Nassau* participating in Desert Storm. Ships such as these, carrying 2,000 troops, their transport, helicopters and aircraft, are hugely versatile, yet represent an all-eggs-in-one-basket vulnerability.** BELOW: **LHAs are named after actions significant to US Marine Corps history. Here, the *Saipan* (LHA-2) has her communications antennas lowered for flight operations.**

25,401-tonne/25,000-ton *Tarawa*-class LHA (Amphibious Assault Ship), combining the floodable docking well and vehicle deck of an LPD (Landing Platform, Dock) with an LPH's hangar space and flight deck. These could accommodate four Landing Craft, Utility, (LCU) in the well, together with smaller landing craft under davits.

A Tarawa was soon involved in satisfactory operation of Marine Corps V/STOL Harriers, while under development at the time was the fast Landing Craft, Air Cushion (LCAC). Both were seen as having potential and the LHA was stretched to accommodate them.

The resulting Helicopter/Dock Landing Ship (LHD) of the Wasp class weighs in at over 28,449 tonnes/28,000 tons. Still designed around the transportation of a marine battalion, her well is dimensioned to accommodate three LCACs and her flight deck is strengthened for routine V/STOL operation. In addition, she was designed with an eye to conversion to anti-submarine warfare (ASW) duties.

With the demise of the commando carriers in the 1970s, Britain deployed only the *Hermes*, which doubled as an ASW carrier, and a pair of LPDs. However, with the catastrophic run-down of the British merchant fleet it is no longer possible to simply charter suitable ships in an emergency. Considerable investment has, therefore, been required to create a coherent assault squadron comprising the *Ocean,* the two Albions and four *Bay*-class auxiliaries, the latter fitted with wells.

Carriers in the Falklands War

When, in April 1982, the Royal Navy had urgently to form a task group to take an expeditionary force to reclaim the invaded Falkland Islands, only two carriers remained to it, neither capable of deploying high-performance, CTOL aircraft. These, the *Invincible* and *Hermes*, sailed on April 5 with a total of 20 Sea Harriers and 28 Sea King helicopters. Ahead lay the whole hostile Argentine air force with one carrier of its own.

Following regrouping of participating ships at Ascension Island the now-organized Carrier Task Group 317.8 (CTG 317.8) left for the 322km/200-mile Maritime Exclusion Zone declared about the islands. Further aircraft, including RAF ground-attack Harriers and troop-carrying Chinook helicopters, followed aboard roll-on, roll-off (ro-ro) merchantmen.

On April 25, with deceptive ease, a small Argentine garrison on South Georgia was persuaded to surrender, four ship's helicopters having sunk a submarine alongside their jetty.

On May 1, the task group entered the Argentine-declared exclusion zone and set about establishing sea superiority, opening with bombardments of selected targets. The carriers remained further to the north-east, their distance attracting endless ribaldry from those at the firing end. Nonetheless, the operation's success depended upon air cover and the loss of

TOP: **Despite furious fitting-out work at Wallsend, second-of-class *Illustrious* was completed just too late to participate in the Falklands War. She is seen here (nearest) taking over from the hard-worked *Invincible* in September 1982.**

ABOVE: **A Type 42's best defence against an Exocet was to deflect it by passive means. The *Sheffield* reacted too slowly to a clear warning of an approaching air-launched missile.**

either carrier would have enforced its abandonment. This could not be risked.

The short-legged Sea Harriers had some local advantage as the enemy A-4 Skyhawks, Daggers and Mirages had to undertake a 1,127km/700-mile round trip, from the mainland, which left them no loiter time over the islands. The island-based Pucara ground-attack aircraft were no match for the British fighters.

One of three nuclear submarines in the area, HMS *Conqueror*, torpedoed and sank the Argentine cruiser *General Belgrano* on May 2. A controversial action, it was designed,

> "Every single Falklands casualty ... 778 is the official total — spent some part of his life in a helicopter."
> Surgeon Cdr Rick Jolley, interview of October 24, 1989

"You learn down here to weep silently in your cabin at man's folly."
Rev Charles E. Stewart, Scottish Free Church chaplain
to HMS *Hermes* at the Falklands

successfully, to establish a clear moral ascendancy. The enemy fleet, including its carrier *25 de Mayo*, played no further part in the campaign.

The Argentine air force, on the other hand, redoubled its efforts. Ship after ship was hit by conventional low-level bombing. Many bombs fortunately failed to explode but ships were sunk and others severely damaged.

With a fair measure of sea control established, the army was put ashore on May 21 at San Carlos, nearly 97km/60 miles from its objective, the capital, Port Stanley.

Beyond the range of direct air attack, the enemy air force could reach the carriers only with their Super Etendard fighter-bombers flying to maximum range to release air-launched Exocet anti-ship missiles. In seeking to do this they failed, but succeeded in destroying the large ro-ro *Atlantic Conveyor*, together with her Chinook helicopters. The troops would now have to "yomp" to Port Stanley. This would take time, leaving the navy to hang on with minimal support, 12,875km/8,000 miles from home bases and in the depths of the Southern winter. It was with relief, therefore, that several brisk actions later, troops re-entered Port Stanley on June 14 enforcing the Argentine surrender.

A short but unpleasant war had cost about 1,000 lives, 75 per cent of them Argentine. From all causes, the British lost 10 V/STOL and 24 helicopters. About 100 Argentine aircraft are believed to have failed to return. Four Royal Navy ships, a fleet auxiliary, and a merchantman were sunk.

The Sea Harrier fighters were remarkably successful, as were their Sidewinder air-to-air missiles (AAMs). These aircraft flew over 1,400 defensive sorties, the RAF a further 150 in ground attack. Without the two aircraft carriers, however, they would not have been there.

ABOVE: **A view from *Hermes* of her "minder", the Sea Wolf-armed Type 22 frigate *Broadsword*. Type 22s were also paired with Sea Dart-armed Type 42s to form "missile traps".**

Glossary

AAM Air-to-Air Missile.

AEW Airborne Early Warning.

AS Anti-Submarine.

ASM Air-to-Surface Missile or Anti-Ship Missile.

ASW Anti-Submarine Warfare.

Accelerator Catapult which accelerates a trolley-mounted aircraft.

Aerostat Tethered, non-navigable lighter-than-air craft, e.g. kite balloon.

Anglo-German Naval Agreement (1935) Agreement for German fleet to be built up to fixed proportion of Royal Navy strength. *Inter alia*, this approved two 22,353-tonne/22,000-ton aircraft carriers for the German Navy.

"Arapaho" Proposed means of deploying V/STOL aircraft from large merchantmen by containerization of all associated services.

Arrester (system) A series of (now) retractable transverse wires, engaged by an aircraft's tailhook to bring it to a halt. Historically also fore-and-aft wires in combination with ramps.

Avgas Aviation fuel.

bhp Brake horsepower. Power actually developed by an engine.

Ballast Additional weight put aboard to improve stability, to correct trim or to modify ship movement.

Barrier Flexible entanglement to make emergency arrest of aircraft that has jumped the arrester wires, with minimum damage to aircraft or pilot.

"Batman" *See* Deck Landing Officer.

Beam Width of hull at the waterline at Standard Displacement.

Belt Heavy vertical side armour designed to defeat low-trajectory gunfire.

"Blimp" Non-rigid dirigible. Small airship primarily for coastal duty.

Blister *See* Bulge.

Bulge Watertight compartment(s) added and faired to mainly underwater section of hull to increase buoyancy or to improve stability.

Bunkers Compartments for stowage of fuel.

C3 (C-3) US Maritime Commission designation for a cargo ship of between 137–152m/450–500ft waterline length and carrying less than 100 passengers.

C-in-C Commander-in-Chief.

CAP Combat Air Patrol. A ship or squadron's organic air cover.

CIWS Close-In Weapon System, e.g. Goalkeeper.

CMB Coastal Motor Boat. The Motor Torpedo Boat (MTB) was a derivative.

CTG Carrier Task Group.

CTOL Conventional Take-Off and Land.

CV Aircraft Carrier.

CVA Attack Aircraft Carrier.

CVE Escort Carrier.

CVL Light Aircraft Carrier.

CVN Nuclear-Propelled Aircraft Carrier.

CVS Anti-Submarine Aircraft Carrier.

Calibre Bore diameter of gun barrel. Also measure of barrel length, e.g. a 3in 70 will be 3 x 70 = 210in in length.

Camber Athwartships curve or rise of a ship's deck.

Cantilever Overhung structure supported at only one side or end.

Casing (funnel) Outer plating surrounding exhaust end of uptake.

Catapult Device to accelerate an aircraft directly.

Deadweight (tonnage) Actual carrying capacity of a cargo ship, expressed in tons of 2,240lb. Abbreviated to dwt.

Deck Landing Officer (or "Batman") Crew man who guides landing aircraft with visual signals. Largely superseded by Mirror Landing Sight.

Derrick Pivoted spar, rigged with winches, for lifting loads.

Dirigible Powered, navigable airship. May be framed (rigid) or unframed (non-rigid).

Displacement, full load or "deep" Weight of ship (in tons of 2,240lb) when fully equipped, stored and fuelled.

Displacement, standard Weight of ship less fuel and other deductions allowed by treaty.

Draught (or Draft) Mean depth of water in which a ship may float freely.

ECM Electronic Countermeasures.

ESM Electronic Support Measures.

Fleet Air Arm (FAA) Air Wing of the Royal Navy.

Fighter Catapult Ship Naval-manned equivalent of Catapult Armed Merchantman (CAM).

Flare Outward curvature of hull plating.

Fleet Train World War II term for Afloat Support. The assembly of auxiliary vessels which keep a fleet supplied and operational.

Floatplane Same as Seaplane. Aircraft supported on water by external floats.

Flying boat Aircraft supported on water by its own hull, and steadied by wingtip floats.

Freeboard For aircraft carriers, the vertical distance from waterline (at standard displacement) to the flight deck.

Gross registered tons (grt) Measure of volumetric capacity of a merchant ship. One gross ton equals 100cu ft (2.83m³) of reckonable space.

Grand Fleet Title carried by the British battle fleet during World War I.

HAPAG Acronym for Hamburg-America Line.

Heavier-than-air Applied to aircraft supported by lift generated by airflow over horizontal surfaces.

High Sea(s) Fleet Title carried by German battle fleet during World War I.

Horsepower Unit of power equal to 746 watts.

ICBM Intercontinental Ballistic Missile.

ihp Indicated horsepower. Specifically the power delivered by the pistons of a reciprocating steam engine.

JSF Joint Strike Fighter.

Kite balloon Aerostat deployed by ships for observation purposes.

LCA Landing Craft, Assault. 12.5m/41.1ft, 35 troops. Carried under davits.

LCAC Landing Craft, Air Cushion. 26.8m/87.9ft, 61 tonnes/60 tons capacity. Carried in well.

LCT Landing Craft, Tank. 58.5m/192ft, 203 tonnes/200 tons capacity. Sea-going.

LCU Landing Craft, Utility. 41m/134.7ft, 145 tonnes/143 tons capacity. Carried in well.

LCVP Landing Craft, Vehicle, Personnel. 10.9m/35.8ft, 35 troops. Carried under davits.

LHA Amphibious Assault Ship.

LHD Helicopter/Dock Landing Ship.

LPD Amphibious Transport, Dock.

LPH Amphibious Assault Helicopter Carrier.

LSD Dock Landing Ship.

Landplane Aircraft with wheeled undercarriage, as opposed to Seaplane with floats.

Length (bp) Length between perpendiculars. Customarily the distance between forward extremity of waterline at standard displacement and the forward side of rudder post. For American warships, lengths on designed waterline and between perpendiculars are synonymous.

Length (oa) Length overall.

Length (wl) Length, waterline. Waterline length at standard displacement.

Lighter-than-air Applied to aircraft whose lift depends upon the buoyancy of gas.

London Treaty (First of 1929–30 and Second of 1935–36) Treaties seeking to reaffirm but to modify the terms of the Washington Treaty (1921–22).

NATO North Atlantic Treaty Organization.

NDL Norddeutscher Lloyd, Bremen.

PDMS Point Defence Missile System. Short-range missile system, often on common mount with a rapid-fire gun, for "last-ditch" defence.

Pallisade Windbreak erected to screen launch area on early carriers.

Plan "Orange" American war plan for use against Japan.

Protective deck Either flat, or incorporating slopes or pronounced curvature, the protective deck protects spaces beneath from bombs, plunging fire or splinters.

Royal Air Force (RAF) Unified force created in April 1918 through the amalgamation of the RFC and the RNAS.

RFA Royal Fleet Auxiliary. Afloat support ships of the Royal Navy.

RFC Royal Flying Corps. The army's air wing prior to 1918.

RNAS Royal Naval Air Service. The navy's air wing prior to 1918.

SAM Surface-to-Air Missile.

SCS Sea Control Ship.

shp Shaft horsepower. Power at point in shaft ahead of stern gland. Does not include frictional losses in stern gland and A-bracket, if fitted.

SSBN Nuclear-Propelled, Ballistic Missile Submarine.

SSM Surface-to-Surface Missile.

SSN Nuclear-Powered Fleet Submarine.

STOVL Short Take-Off, Vertical Land.

STUFT Ships Taken Up From Trade. Merchant ships chartered for the support of naval requirements.

Seaplane *See* Floatplane.

Sheer Curvature of deckline in fore-and-aft direction, usually upward at either end.

Sided Situated toward sides of ship, usually as opposed to centreline location.

Ski-jump A pronounced upward curvature of forward end of flight deck of a V/STOL carrier. Enhances the effect of short take-off run.

Stability range Total angle through which, from a position of equilibrium, a ship is statically stable.

TF Task Force, e.g. TF38. A group of warships assembled for a specific purpose.

TG Task Group, e.g. TG38.1, TG38.2 etc. The major components of a Task Force.

TU Task Unit, e.g. TU38.1.1, TU38.1.2. The major components of a Task Group.

TSR Torpedo/Spotter/Reconnaissance. Roles for which aircraft such as the Fairey Swordfish were designed.

Trim Amount by which a ship deviates, in the fore-and-aft axis, from her designed draught.

Turbo-electric Propulsion system in which a steam turbine drives an electrical generator. This supplies energy via cable to a propulsion motor coupled to the propeller shaft.

UN United Nations.

Uptake Conduit conducting products of combustion to the funnel.

V/STOL Vertical or Short Take-Off and Land.

Volume critical A ship whose design is driven by needs of space rather than weight, e.g. aircraft carrier.

Warsaw Pact Eastern military bloc, essentially a counter to NATO.

Washington Treaty (c1921–22) Arms limitation agreement that had a profound effect on the development of the aircraft carrier.

Weight critical A ship whose design is driven by considerations of weight rather than space, e.g. a heavily armoured battleship.

Index

Aerospatiale UH-13 Ecureuils, 73
Aichi
  D1A1 (Type 94), 43
  D1A2 (Type 96) "Susie", 43
  D3A1 (Type 90) "Val", 43, 61
  M6A1 Seiren, 41
Akagi, 57
Akron ZRS.4 (airship), 28–9
Albion, 74
Albion (L14) commando carrier, 88–9
Antietam CV-36, 69, 71
Argus
  (I), 6, 19, 34, 38
  (II), 48
Ark Royal
  (I), 12, 13, 14
  (II), 44–5, 49
  (III), 7, 45, 68, 79, 84–5
Armstrong Whitworth (Hawker) Sea Hawk, 74–5, 79
Arromanches, 72, 74
Atlantic Conveyor, 91
Auxiliary carriers, 58–9
Avro 504, 25

Bay class, 89
Bell
  HTL/HUL, 76
Bellau Wood
  CVL-24, 67, 73
  LHA-3, 85
Ben-my-Chree, 14, 15, 19

Besson MB.411 seaplane, 41
Bismarck, sinking of, 34, 42, 48–9
Blackburn
  Buccaneer, 79
  Firebrand, 60
  Roc, 60
  Skua, 42
Boeing
  Apache, 77
  Chinook, 90–1
  F2B, 42
  F3B, 42
  F4B, 42
  FB-2, 42
  FB-5, 42
Bois Belleau (R97), 73
Bonaventure, 73
Boxer
  CV-21, 70, 83, 88
Bristol Scout, 16
British airships 28–9
Bulwark, 74
Bulwark (L15) commando carrier, 76, 84, 88
Bunker Hill CV-17, 65, 76

Cabot CVL-28, 73
Campania (I), 16, 17, 22
Cape Engano, Battle of, 67
Casablanca CVE-55, 58
Caspar-Heinkel U-1 floatplane, 40
Caudron G.III, 13, 21
CH-46 Sea Knight, 88
CH-53 Sea Stallion, 81

Chambers, Captain Washington Irving, 8
Chance-Vought F4U Corsair, 58, 60, 71, 74
Charles de Gaulle, 79
Chaser, 58
Chitose CVL, 67
Churchill, Winston, 8, 18, 19, 21, 24–5
Colossus, 72
Colossus class, 72
Commando Carriers, 75, 88–9
Consolidated
  B-24 Liberator, 59
  PBY Catalina, 49, 53, 62
Constellation CVA-64, 6, 80
Coral Sea CVB-43, 45
Coral Sea, Battle of, 54–5, 56
Courageous, 34, 39
Cunningham, Admiral Andrew, 47, 50–1
Curtiss
  AB-3, 38
  CS, 42
  F9C/O9C Sparrowhawk, 29
  Falcon F8C Helldiver, 43
  F-Type, 13
  Model 24 (CT-1), 19
  R-6L, 19
  SB2C Helldiver, 60–1, 66
  Triad A-1 hydroplane, 8
Curtiss, Glen, 8, 9, 12, 13
CVA-01 (unnamed), 84

Dardanelles campaign, 14, 15, 19
Dassault
  Etendard, 79
  Mirage, 90
  Rafale, 70
  Super Etendard, 91
de Havilland
  (Hawker) Sea Venom, 74
  F.20 Sea Vampire, 78–9
  Vampire I, 79

Dédalo (I), 73
Doolittle Raid, 54–5
Douglas
  A3D Skywarrior (A-3), 68–9, 78
  AD-1 Skyraider (Spad), 60, 71, 80–1
  SBD Dauntless, 42, 55, 56, 60–1
  TBD Devastator, 42, 56

Eagle
  (I), 46
  (II), 74
Ely, Eugene, 8, 9, 12, 38
Empress, 38
Empress (seaplane carrier), 16, 24
Engadine, 16, 22–3, 24
Enterprise
  CV-6, 54, 56–7, 62–3, 64
  CVAN-65, 81
Escort carriers (CVE), 58–9, 71, 88
Essex class, 45, 64, 66, 68, 70–1, 77, 78, 83, 88

Fairey
  Albacore, 60
  Barracuda, 60
  F.17 Campania, 27
  Firefly, 60, 70
  Flycatcher, 42
  Fulmar, 42, 60
  III F, 34–5, 42–3
  Swordfish, 42, 46, 48–9, 50–1, 58–9, 60
Falklands War, 81, 85, 90–1
Fisher, Admiral Sir John ("Jackie"), 6, 7
Fletcher, Rear Admiral Jack, 54–5
Focke-Wulf Fw200 Condor, 58–9
Formidable, 50–1
Forrestal class, 78
Foudre, 13
Franklin D. Roosevelt CVB-42 (CVA-41), 78

Friedrichshafen, 24–5
Friedrichshafen FF-29a,
    40
Furious (I), 17, 25, 27, 38

Gallipoli Peninsula, 14, 15
Glorious, 39
Great Lakes
    BG-1, 42
    TG.2, 42
Grumman
    A-6 Intruder, 78–9
    E-2 Hawkeye (AEW), 69
    F-14 Tomcat, 79, 86
    F2F, 42–3
    F3F, 42–3
    F4F Wildcat (Martlet), 42,
        56, 59, 60–1, 62
    F6F Hellcat, 59, 60–1, 65,
        67, 76
    F7F Tigercat, 60
    F9F Panther, 70, 78
    S-2 Tracker, 73
    TBF/TBM Avenger, 38, 79,
        60, 67, 74
Guadalcanal, 54, 62–3

Halsey, Admiral William F.,
    66–7
Hancock CV-19, 69
Hawker
    GR.1 Harrier, 84
    Osprey, 42
    P.1127 "Kestrel", 84
    Sea Fury, 70
    Sea Harrier, 84, 89,
        90–1
    Sea Hurricane, 60
Hector, 15
Heinkel He 66, 43
Heligoland Bight, 24–5
Hercules, 73
Hermes
    (I), 13, 26
    (II), 84–5, 89, 90
Hiryu, 57
Hiyo, 65
Hornet
    CV-8, 54–5, 56, 62–3
Hosho, 31

I-400 class (submarine),
    41
Iachino, Admiral, 50–1
Inchon LPH-12, 81

Illustrious, 45, 46, 51
Independence
    CVA-62, 78, 83
Independence class, 64
Intrepid CV-11, 68
Invincible, 82, 84–5, 90
Israel Aircraft Industries
    Dagger, 90
Iwo Jima
    LPH-2, 88
Iwo Jima class (LPH), 89

Jellicoe, Admiral John, 11, 16,
    22–3
John C. Stennis CVN-74, 83
Junyo, 63
Jutland, Battle of, 22–3, 31

kamikaze, 67, 83
Karel Doorman (II), 73
Kawanishi
    E7K (Type 94), "Alf", 35
Kitty Hawk CVA-63, 82
Königsberg, 20, 21
Korean War, 70–1, 76–7,
    78–9
Kure, 30
Kurita, Admiral, 66–7
Kwajalein CVE-98, 58

La Fayette (R96), 73, 74
Langley
    CV-1, 38
Lee, Vice Admiral Willis A.,
    64
Lexington
    CV-16, 69
    CV-2, 33, 34, 54–5
Lexington (CV-2) class,
    35
Leyte CV-32, 78
Leyte Gulf, Battle of, 66–7
Light Fleet Carriers (CVL),
    70–1, 72–3, 74, 88
Lockheed
    Merlin F-35 (JSF), 79, 85
Los Angeles ZR.3 (airship),
    29

M2 (submarine), 40
Macon ZRS.5 (airship), 29
Magnificent, 72
Majestic, 72
Majestic class, 72
Malta, 44

Martin
    MS-1, 41
    T3M, 42
    T4M, 42
Matapan, Battle of, 34, 42,
    48, 50–1
McDonnell
    F2H Banshee, 77, 78
    F3H Demon, 78
    FH-1 Phantom I, 78
McDonnell Douglas
    A-4 Skyhawks, 69, 78, 81,
        90–1
    F/A-18 Hornet, 79
    F4H Phantom II (F-4), 6,
        78–9
McDonnell Douglas/BAE
    Systems AV-8A/B
    Harrier II, 84, 89, 90–1
Melbourne, 72
Merchant Aircraft Carriers
    (MAC), 73
Merlin helicopter, 77
Midway, Battle of, 56–7
Midway class, 60, 78
Midway CVB-41, 45, 69
Mikoyan-Gurevich MiG-15, 74
Minas Gerais, 73
Mitchell, Brigadier General
    William "Billy", 36–7
Mitscher, Vice Admiral
    Marc A., 55, 64–5, 66–7,
        82
Mitsubishi
    A5M4 (Type 96) "Claude",
        43
    A6M (Type O) "Zeke" or
        "Zero", 43, 61, 67
    B1M1 (Type 13), 31
    B1M1 (Type 13), 43
    B2M1 (Type 89), 43
    J2M Raiden, 61

MV-22 Osprey tilt-rotor
    aircraft, 77

Nagato class, 33
Nagumo Chuichi, Admiral,
    52–3, 56–7, 62–3
Nakajima
    A1N1 (Type 3), 42
    A2N1 (Type 90), 42
    A2N2, 31
    A4N1 (Type 95), 43
    B5N1, 61
    B5N2 (Type 97) "Kate", 43,
        52, 57, 61, 63
    B6N Tenzen, 61
Nassau
    LHA-4, 88–9
Nieuport Two-seater, 15
Nimitz, Admiral Chester, 56
Nishimura, Admiral, 66
North American
    A.J. Savage, 68
    A-5 Vigilante, 6
    B-25 Mitchell, 54–5
Northrop BT, 42

Ocean, 70, 74–5, 78–9
Ocean (L12), 89
Ozawa Jisaburo, Admiral,
    64–5, 66

Parnall Peto floatplane, 40
Pearl Harbor, attack on, 35,
    52–3, 54
Pegasus, 17
Perseus, 69
Pfalz Otto biplane, 21
Philippine Sea, Battle of,
    64–5, 66, 82
Philippine Sea CV-47, 83
Plasecki Vertol HUP-2, 77
Powerful, 73

Queen, 59

Ranger
  CV-4, 44–5, 54
Renown, 49
Riviera, 16, 24
Rutland, Squadron
    Commander Frederick J.
    ("of Jutland"), 16, 22–3,
    31

S-1 (submarine), 40
Saipan, 64–5
Saipan LHA-2, 89
Samar, Battle of, 66–7
Samson, Wing Commander
    Charles Rummney, 8–9,
    15
Santa Cruz, Battle of, 62–3
Saratoga
  CV-3, 33, 34–5, 63
Scheer, Admiral, 22–3
Sea King, 73, 84, 90
Searcher, 59
Sempill Mission, 30–1
Shenandoah ZR.1 (airship), 29
Shoho, 54–5
Shokaku, 7, 52, 54–5, 62–3,
    65
Short
  166, 12, 14
  184, 14, 15, 22–3, 27
  827/830, 21
  Brothers, 26
  Folder, 18
  S.27, 8
  S.38, 9
  S.64, 13
  Seaplane, 21
Sikorsky
  H03S-1, 76
  HNS-1 (R-48), 77

HR25, 88
HUS Seahorse, 89
R-4 Hoverfly I, 76
S-51, 71, 76
S-55, 71, 77
S-58, 77
VS-300, 76
VS-316 (R-4), 76
Slinger, 12, 38
Solomons CVE-67, 59
Somerville, Admiral, 49
Sopwith
  1½-Strutter, 16, 27
  2F.1 Camel, 10, 17, 25, 27
  2F.2 Camel, 16, 42
  Baby, 26–7
  Pup, 16, 17, 25, 26–7, 31,
    38–9
  Schneider, 15, 26–7
  T.1 Cuckoo, 18–19, 27, 31
  Tabloid, 26
  Type "C", 18
Sopwith, Thomas, 18–19
Spruance, Admiral
    Raymond A., 56–7, 64–5
Sueter, Captain Murray, 18–19
Suez, 74–5
Supermarine
  Attacker, 79
  Scimitar, 79
  Seafire, 60, 70–1
  Spiteful, 79
Surcouf (submarine), 40–1
Surigao Strait, 66
Sydney, 16, 70–1, 72

Taiho, 65
Takagi Takao, Vice Admiral,
    54–5
Taranto, raid on, 42, 46–7
Tarawa class, 85, 89
Tarawa LHA-1, 89

Terrible, 72
Theseus, 71, 74–5
Thetis Bay CVE-90 (CVHA-1),
    88
Tondern Zeppelin base, 17,
    25
Triumph, 69, 70
Trumpeter, 59
Tsushima, Battle of, 30
Tyrwhitt, Commodore, 17, 24

United States CVA-58, 78

Valiant, 47
Valley Forge CV-45, 70
*Veinticinco de Mayo (25 de
    Mayo)*, 91
Venerable, 73
Vengeance, 73
Victorious, 48
Vietnam War, 80–1
Vikrant, 73
Vindex, 16
Vittorio Veneto (battleship),
    50–1
Vought F8U Crusader (F8), 6,
    69, 78, 80

Wakamiya, 13, 31
Warrior, 22, 73
Washington Treaty (1921–22),
    32–3, 44

Watanabe
  E14Y1 ("Glen"), 41
  E9W1 ("Slim"), 41
West Virginia, 53
Westland
  Dragonfly, 76
  Sycamore, 75
  Wasp HAS.1, 77
  Wessex, 76, 77
  Whirlwind, 75, 77
  Wyvern, 68, 74
Wright, Orville, 6

Yak-141, 85
Yalu, Battle of the, 30
Yamamoto Isoroku, Admiral,
    53, 56–7
Yokosuka
  B3Y1 (Type 92), 43
  B4Y1 (Type 96) "Jean", 43
  D4Y1 Suisei, 61
  E6Y1, 41
Yorktown
  CV-5, 54–5, 56–7, 65

Zeppelin, 10–11, 16–17,
    22–3, 24–5, 26, 28–9, 58
Zeppelin, Graf Ferdinand von,
    10, 11
ZR.2 (airship), 29
Zuiho, 62–3
Zuikaku, 7, 54, 62–3, 65, 67

Acknowledgements

Research for the pictures used to illustrate this book was carried out by Ted Nevill of TRH Pictures. Ted Nevill would like to thank all those who contributed to the research and supply of these images, in particular the staff at the Photographic Section of the Naval Historical Center, Washington, DC, and at Still Pictures at the National Archives at College Park, Maryland, USA.

The artworks used in this book were drawn by Jan Suermondt for Cody Images or supplied by ArtTech. Photographs and other illustrations were supplied by Cody Images with help from ArtTech, Chrysalis Image Library, Leo Marriott, Robert Hunt Picture Library and the following. Every effort has been made to acknowledge the pictures properly; however, we apologize if there are any unintentional omissions, which will be corrected in future editions.

AgustaWestland: 79.
BAE Systems: 7 bottom right; 88 top.